The national leaders who receive their university training in the United States could well be the strongest witness for Christ across our globe—*if* they are led to Christ. This excellent book provides the know-how to make it happen—to God's glory—through each of us.

Dr. Ted W. Engstrom—President Emeritus
World Vision

Many developing countries send their brightest young people to spend their formative years in our universities. The few years they spend here can affect the direction of a whole country when they return home. Christians who recognize these facts see the vast potential for good in reaching out to foreign students during their often lonely days among us. This book shows churches how to reach out to the "stranger within our gates" and exciting ways of reaching out to whole countries at minimal expense with maximum effectiveness.

Dr. D. Stuart Briscoe—Senior Pastor
Elmbrook Church, Brookfield, Wisconsin

Thinking globally is more than a maxim, it is a mandate. *The World at Your Door* helps us touch the heart of the world and brings the best of its thinkers within reach.

Dr. Ravi Zacharias
Ravi Zacharias International Ministries

What a unique blending—this book's challenges are exciting, its storytelling style is captivating, the breath of God's Spirit in every chapter is enlivening, and the practical content is confidence-building.

Dr. R. Allan Dunbar—President
Puget Sound Christian College

Ministering to international students should be one of the highest priorities of the Church in America. This significant book will help every thinking Christian to not only understand the *should* of such a strategic ministry, but also the *how*.

Dr. Paul A. Cedar—Chairman
Mission America

This volume recognizes an incredible opportunity that God has given to the twentieth-century American church. The time is right, the need urgent, and the opportunity vast. I am happy to commend this work.

Adrian Rogers—Senior Pastor
Bellevue Baptist Church, Cordova, Tennessee

International students studying among us are perhaps more open and vulnerable than they will ever be for the rest of their lives. This book will open your eyes, stir your heart, and motivate you to get involved in one of the most critical ministries of this generation—that is, introducing a student to Jesus Christ. This event will not only change a person for eternity, it could shake a nation for God.

Wayde I. Goodall
National Coordinator of Ministerial Enrichment
The General Council of the Assemblies of God

The World at Your Door presents a picture too few Christians understand. The future leaders of the world study in the United States. Few of them ever step inside an American home, fewer yet in the home of a believer, and fewer yet in the home of a believer who knows how to have a long-term witness for the Gospel with these students. This is a *must* for every Christian living near a university.

Dr. Jerry E. White
General Director and International President
The Navigators

The World at Your Door could measure a seven on the Richter scale to the sleepy believer who has a heart for missions but thinks the world is too far away.

Pastor Jack Hayford
The Church on the Way, Van Nuys, California

This book is long overdue—informative, challenging, and practical help in understanding the scope of the international student population in our country and the spiritual potential they represent. Little do most of us realize that this unreached, highly motivated group is right at our doorstep in the major universities of our country.

Cliff Barrows
Billy Graham Evangelistic Association

An estimated 554,000 scholars and students in America from abroad will return home to almost 200 countries. This, by far, is one of the best-leveraged dollar investments in world evangelism today. *The World at Your Door* is a strategic book long-awaited in the missions community.

Dick Eastman—International President
Every Home for Christ International

This book is the most concise, practical guide available to reaching out to the mission field at our doorstep. It doesn't give you a guilt trip. It makes missions real and relational, a possibility for all of us.

Lars Dunberg—International President
International Bible Society

Do you see all the students who have happened to find themselves away from home and near your front door? What is your commitment to those who may never have known the peace of Christ? *The World at Your Door* will open your eyes to the reality of their need and place your life in their pathway.

H. B. London Jr.
Vice-President, Ministry Outreach/Pastoral Ministries
Focus on the Family

This is wise reading for anyone concerned to bring Christ to these future world leaders. It is a worthy work, and thus worthy of the deep commitment of God's people who are concerned for the evangelization of the world.

Dr. Lewis A. Drummond
Billy Graham Professor of Evangelism
and Church Growth
Beeson Divinity School, Samford University

Too often we have viewed missions with binoculars scanning distant lands and we have failed to see the unique opportunities at our front door. Tom Phillips opens our eyes to see the vast mission field of international students in our midst.

David Burnham
Burnham Ministries International

No ministry today offers greater returns for the kingdom than working with university students. This book tells us how to reap the harvest. A tremendously uplifting challenge!

Dr. Robert E. Coleman—Dean
Trinity Evangelical Divinity School

American Christians have a wonderful opportunity: international students come to us! *The World at Your Door* offers a compelling case for ministering to these hungry learners.

Roger Cross—President
Youth for Christ/USA

Fulfilling the Great Commission begins on our doorstep—especially when it comes to reaching international students with the Gospel. Readers will find *The World at Your Door* truly helpful.

Franklin Graham
Samaritan's Purse

You don't have to drop everything, learn a foreign language, and fly to a distant land to impact key national leaders. They're knocking at the door. Thousands of students will become national leaders. Most of them will spend four to five years studying in the United States and never be inside an American home, much less a Christian one. That's terrible! Answer the doorbell.

Dr. Joseph C. Aldrich—President
Multnomah Bible College and Biblical Seminary

This remarkable book is telescopic in its reach to the most remote areas on earth, and microscopic in its focus on the vital, critical student population of this world. Truly, the ministry to international students is in many respects the most strategic and most visionary "window of opportunity" open to Christian evangelism on the threshold of the twenty-first century.

Dr. D. James Kennedy—Senior Minister
Coral Ridge Presbyterian Church

The World at Your Door is an exciting and challenging ministry tool that the church has long awaited. A must-read for every pastor, church leader, and missions-minded layperson.

John Maxwell—Founder
INJOY

The Navigators are wholeheartedly committed to sharing the love of Christ with international students God has providentially placed in this country. We want to endorse and support International Students, Incorporated and the strategic part they are playing in advancing the cause of Christ. This is a great book on how you can play a part in God's great plan of redemption.

Dr. Terry Taylor—President
The Navigators

A personal international ministry for Christ without travel? It sounds impossible, yet I've seen it happen. I've seen its profound impact on individuals . . . on the church . . . on faraway places. Tom Phillips and Bob Norsworthy have seen it happen too. It is their calling to make it happen. They explain it well in this book.

Max Meyer—President
Mission Aviation Fellowship

This is a book for those who are made anxious by the word "evangelism" but who love a party! It's a call to be festive and welcoming, to reach out with friendship to the international student at your door. Full of God's strategies—practical suggestions and motivational encouragement.

Pastor Burdette (Bud) Palmberg
The International Church of Luzern, Switzerland

Promise Keepers believes that one of the results of God's Spirit moving in the lives of men will be mobilization for ministry. Men, here's a way to lead your family in helping fulfill the Great Commission through foreign missions on your doorstep!

Randy Phillips
Promise Keepers

The last command of our Leader was "Go into the world and make disciples." Most of us didn't know how to carry out that mandate. Now Christ says, "Okay, then, I'll send the world to you. Now make disciples." *The World at Your Door* tells us how to salute and say, "Yes, Sir!" and go out and do it.

Dr. Haddon Robinson
Gordon-Conwell Theological Seminary

Tom Phillips has his finger on the great mission field on our doorstep—that of international students. What he models for us is creative, effective ministry.

Dr. John Huffman Jr.—Senior Minister
St. Andrew's Presbyterian Church, Newport Beach, California

This book speaks to a virtually unrecognized opportunity to evangelize the world. Every Christian ought to seriously consider whether or not this kind of outreach to international students would be a place to invest their kingdom resources.

Daniel Southern—President
American Tract Society

The student from overseas in your community will become a leader in his or her own country. To develop a friendship with and be an example of Christ's love to that student could not only change a life but impact an entire nation. Please read this book!

Dr. Larry E. Keyes—President
OC International

Many of us understand that reaching international students is strategic, as they represent the future leadership of their home countries. But few of us know how or where to begin. This book takes away the mystery and provides practical, specific help to get into this exciting ministry.

Paul D. Stanley—Vice-President
The Navigators

Do you live near a college or university? God may have strategically placed you there for purposes of his kingdom—and Tom Phillips and Bob Norsworthy explain why. This is an informative, practical how-to book with which anyone can identify.

Richard A. (Dick) Armstrong—Senior Vice-President
The ServiceMaster Company

Jesus tells us that when the harvest is ripe, many laborers are needed. International students in the U.S. are usually much more receptive to the Gospel than they would be in their home countries. You can be one of God's laborers in this ripe harvest field, and *The World at Your Door* is a crash course to provide you the basic training that you need for this exciting task.

Dr. C. Peter Wagner—Professor of Church Growth
Fuller Theological Seminary

The World at Your Door is a primer for the average American Christian on how he or she can impact the world, even without leaving their neighborhood. This is efficient and effective evangelism at its best.

John Woodyard—Program Director
M. J. Murdock Charitable Trust

Learn the secrets of sending missionaries overseas who require no visas, no foreign language training, no cross-cultural orientation, and seldom any financial support. Unbelievable? Read *The World at Your Door* and get involved in the adventure of global missions beginning at your door. A must-read for all missionary-minded Christians and churches.

Dr. T. V. Thomas—International Minister-at-Large
Every Home for Christ International

The World at Your Door will move you to open the door of your home and heart to international students.

Pastor James O. Rose—Senior Pastor
Grace Covenant Church, Austin, Texas

The World at Your Door

Dr. Tom Phillips
Bob Norsworthy

with W. Terry Whalin

BETHANY HOUSE PUBLISHERS
MINNEAPOLIS, MINNESOTA 55438

Published by Bethany House Publishers
A Ministry of Bethany Fellowship, Inc.
11300 Hampshire Avenue South
Minneapolis, Minnesota 55438

Printed in the United States of America.

Library of Congress Cataloging-in-Publication Data

Phillips, Tom.
    The world at your door : reaching international students in your home, church, and school / by Tom Phillips, Bob Norsworthy with W. Terry Whalin.
        p.   cm.
    Includes bibliographical references.
    ISBN 1-55661-964-2 (pbk.)
    1. Church work with foreign students—United States.
I. Norsworthy, Bob.   II. Whalin, W. Terry.   III. Title.
BV4447.P55   1997
259'.24—dc21
                                                            97-21028
                                                                CIP

The unwavering support of my wife, Ouida, has made this book possible as well as the many years of ministry for our Lord. Thank you, dear, for being the best partner in service together for Christ.

This book is also dedicated to my loving parents, Johnny and Lorene Phillips, and children, Cara, Molly, and Matt, whose support has been my encouragement in ministry.

Tom

_____

This book is dedicated to my wife, Cindi, my life partner and best friend. You are the best gift God has ever given me in this life. Thank you for teaching me about joy, laughter, and love. May we serve Jesus and build his kingdom until he takes us home.

It is also dedicated to my three wonderful children, Leisa, Joel, and Danielle. I am extremely proud of each of you. May you seek above all else to know and love Jesus all of your days. I love you and thank you for the time you give up to let Mom and I serve Jesus.

Bob

_____

Christine, you've helped turn this book into a reality through your constant belief and love. Thank you.

Terry

93855

DR. TOM PHILLIPS is President of International Students, Incorporated, and a popular speaker around the world. He was senior crusade director of counseling and follow-up with the Billy Graham Evangelistic Association for twenty years. Tom and his wife, Ouida, live in Colorado, and have three children, Cara, Molly, and Matthew.

BOB NORSWORTHY is Vice-President of ministries for International Students, Incorporated, overseeing ministry to international students on nearly 300 campuses in the United States as well as the development of ISI's international overseas ventures. A graduate of Multnomah School of the Bible, Bob served as a pastor and businessman before his twelve years of service with ISI. Living in Colorado, Bob and his wife, Cindi, have three children, Leisa, Joel, and Danielle.

W. TERRY WHALIN is President of Whalin and Associates, an independent editorial and writing service. He has written more than forty-five books, including numerous biographies, children's books, and coauthored books. In addition, Terry has written hundreds of magazine articles in over fifty publications. Terry and his wife, Christine, live in Colorado.

Acknowledgments

We wish to express our deep appreciation to all of the ISI staff who have worked diligently with us to secure the wonderful testimonies that are expressed throughout the book as well as all of the ISI team who have written ISI witnessing, discipleship, and training materials in the past from which some of the material in this book was gleaned. Further, Dr. Charles Riggs was an inspiration to us.

Also, our thanks to all of those who are servant leaders in the Christian community and endorsed the book, reflecting its potential impact in the church. We believe that the ministry to the future leaders and executives of our world is the most strategic, evangelistic, reproductive ministry facing the church today. It affords us the greatest amount of leverage for the investment—personally, economically, and spiritually.

Our thanks to all who have stood with us in the development of this tool for the sake of the growth of the kingdom through those who will impact their nations for Christ when they return home.

We want especially to acknowledge Terry Whalin, who has labored diligently and faithfully to help us write this work.

We also acknowledge the sovereign work of God both through the ages and today. By his hand he moves the peoples of the earth where he wills, lifts up nations, peoples, and leaders, and has led the leaders of tomorrow to our nation today. We are privileged to be his servants for such a time as this.

Acknowledgments

Foreword

When I ministered with Youth for Christ, I became friends with Bob Finley who, in 1953, launched a full-time ministry called International Students, Incorporated. I was honored to serve on his board of advisors. I told Bob, "Every Christian in America should help reach international students for Christ." In 1957, during the tremendous New York Crusade in Madison Square Garden, Bob brought a number of international students to the meetings who were able to hear the Good News about Jesus Christ.

Today, my good friend Tom Phillips is the president of International Students, Incorporated. For over twenty years, Tom worked shoulder to shoulder with me in organizing evangelistic crusades nationally and internationally. Now he leads one of the most strategic organizations in its efforts to evangelize international students.

Over half a million students come from around the globe to study in the United States—right in our own backyard. As we develop friendships with these future leaders and executives, we have an opportunity to reach our world for Christ. When these students complete their education and return to their homelands, they assume leadership in international corporations and national institutions. Or, they become political leaders, influencing thousands. Unfortunately, during their time in the U.S., over 70 percent of these students never enter an American home or visit a place of worship.

You hold a new tool in your hands to help you take advantage of a wonderful evangelistic opportunity. First, you will discover how this ministry is simple and uncomplicated. Then, step-by-step, you can learn how to develop international friends. Finally, you can gain the skills and insight to lead a student to a personal relationship with Jesus Christ.

Everyone can benefit from the guidance in this book. As you reach out to these potential world leaders at your doorstep, your own Christian life will be strengthened. God will use you as an instrument of peace for the nations. And you don't have to go to the other side of the globe to have an impact.

You might be the person that God uses to bring the next world leader to a personal relationship with Jesus Christ. Or, your relationship will cause this person to be more open to spiritual truth through your expression of the love of Jesus Christ.

I pray that God will use this book to draw many people into the kingdom of God through our Lord Jesus.

—Billy Graham

Preface

Some years ago, when I was in graduate school, my wife was working as a teacher at an inner city high school. She was one of only three white teachers among several thousand students and a couple hundred staff.

One year, one of her colleagues invited us to participate in a family Thanksgiving celebration. We had gone out to dinner several times with the host couple and had always had a good time. Newlyweds at the time, we were living in a small apartment, so it sounded like a great chance to escape our confining quarters and limited culinary talents to gorge ourselves on fine food and fellowship with people we liked. We were told to expect a true family gathering: probably 30 relatives or more. We would be the only outsiders present.

For me, this would be a memorable cultural experience. Our hosts were African-American, and though I had some black friends and had many working relationships with black professionals, I had never been in their homes. I had many preconceived notions about what the day would be like. As it turned out, my predictions were not even in the ball park.

We arrived at their front door with gifts in hand and smiles on our faces. The six hours that followed were unlike anything I had ever experienced before. Everything was different—the language, the customs, the relationships, and the food. Even the prayer before the meal was different. It was a great day, not only for learning, but for being with warm, loving, accepting people. My life was forever changed. I grew in ways that never would have been possible if I had not been invited to share in the world of that family that day.

Common Scenario

My experience is but a microcosm of what could be happening in the lives of half a million visitors to the United States. I am speaking of college students who travel here from other nations to earn their degrees. Although I was a graduate student at the time of the above cited experience, I had only a limited understanding of significant segments of the American culture and the people who comprise this diverse nation. Think of what it must be like for a foreign student coming to America to be educated. Many do not speak our language well. They arrive here with a mindset of a different culture, with likely no preexisting relationships, and with a completely different orientation to resources. All they know about America is what they have seen on TV or read in their homeland publications—and much of that information is skewed by the mass media, and filtered through the lens of international politics.

Most important, the vast majority of visiting students enter our country as non-Christians. They have ideas and perceptions of what Christians and Christianity are about, but those perceptions, like their ideas about our culture, may be wildly inaccurate.

Yes, there are hundreds of seminars and conferences about Christianity they could attend. There are tens of thousands of Christian churches that would welcome these students on a Sunday morning, and there are millions of Christian adults throughout America who may be willing to tell these young people about Christ. But realistically, what are the chances of the typical foreign student registering for a Christian seminar, visiting a Christian church, or initiating a personal relationship with a Christian adult? In truth, there is a huge invisible wall isolating international students from mainstream Christianity. They do not know how to penetrate that barrier. Nor is it their responsibility to do so.

A Glorious Opportunity

As believers living in America, we have an incredible opportunity to influence the lives of this world's emerging generation of influencers. International students sent to America are typically the best and the brightest their countries have to offer. While American high schoolers think of college as their first extended taste of freedom and independence, of adventure and romance, or even academic exploration, for the international student studying in the U.S., it is a very special, highly sought-after prize. They are the future leaders, the chosen ones. And their training in the U.S. will shape the ways they lead.

We are doing them a terrible disservice if we allow them to glean what our professors, books, and research have to offer, but do not expose them to what our faith has to offer. Imagine the impact we could have as disciples of Jesus Christ on the spiritual, moral, and intellectual future of humanity. We have the unique opportunity of building relationships with these fledgling leaders and exposing them to Christianity in its many facets and in a natural setting. And yet the authors of this book tell us that we are squandering this phenomenal privilege of penetrating numerous cultures around the world for Christ.

The type of outreach opportunities described herein do not require travel, large financial investment, uprooting our families, or even substantial training. They do require our being committed to our faith and sharing that faith in genuine and authentic ways with international students, inviting them into our homes and into our lives. Many of these students come from nations that are closed to missionaries, Christian churches, and other forms of evangelism. But while they are visiting America, the only obstacle to American Christians touching the lives of these future international leaders is our own lack of effort to reach out to them.

The authors remind us that we do not need the spiritual gift of evangelism to influence international students. They are seeking hospitality, not a Hollywood experience. We don't have to have a clever evangelistic strategy or presentation prepared. We do need to love Jesus and want to share that love with others in a comfortable, appropriate manner. The authors will help you understand how to make the transition from unaware and uninvolved to caring and connecting.

Did you know that most international students will receive their degrees and leave America without ever having stepped foot into an American home? In his wisdom and compassion, God has brought the mission field right to our door and affords us the outreach opportunities of a lifetime. The question is, are you and I courageous and committed enough to exploit that opportunity for the glory of God?

—George Barna

BOUNCE THIS IDEA OFF OF YOU
To get the opinion of another person.

Other idiom expressions are spread throughout this book for illustration and humor!

Contents

ONE

A Disguised Opportunity

*"Though I am free and belong to no man, I make myself a
slave to everyone, to win as many as possible. To the Jews I
became like a Jew, to win the Jews. To those under the law I
became like one under the law (though I myself am not
under the law), so as to win those under the law. To those
not having the law I became like one not having the law
(though I am not free from God's law but am under
Christ's law), so as to win those not having the law. To the
weak I became weak, to win the weak. I have become all
things to all men so that by all possible means I might save
some. I do all this for the sake of the gospel,
that I may share in its blessings."*

1 Corinthians 9:19–23

Sometimes opportunity knocks at our door but is so disguised we don't
see the potential.

In 1941, a young father in El Salvador won the national lottery. It
changed the course of history for his youngest son, Napoleon. The young
man traveled with his older brother on a bus from his country to South
Bend, Indiana, home of the University of Notre Dame. In St. Louis, the
pair went into a bar, and someone asked them where they were going.
They answered, "We're going to Notre Dame."

One of the men laughed, "Looks like Notre Dame's importing Latin-
American football players to beat Army and Navy." The brothers were
surprised that a school would be best known for its athletics. Napoleon
tried out for the football team and was flattened seconds after someone

tossed him the football. He knew very little about the American sport.

In his autobiography, *Duarte: My Story*, Napoleon tells about his first class, "Christian Virtues," taught by Father Theodore Hesburgh, a young priest beginning his teaching career. Napoleon listened to the lecture but couldn't understand anything about philosophy or ethics. He leaned over and whispered to his friend Cordova, asking what was being said.

The nervous professor suddenly stopped his class and pointed at the young man asking, "What's your name?"

"Napoleon Duarte."

"Well, Nappy, if you continue talking in class, I'm going to throw you out the window!" Father Hesburgh said. After class, the priest motioned for Duarte to stay. "Why were you talking in class?"

In his best English, acquired mainly during that week, Napoleon said, "To understand what you say, I need help." Father Hesburgh softened his attitude and decided to outline his lecture each day in Italian. This language was closer to Spanish and helped Duarte work to complete the course. He worked hard and eventually earned an engineering degree, while also taking on odd jobs in a laundry, an ice cream factory, and washing windows. Napoleon Duarte returned to his native country and became involved in politics. Many years later this young man served two terms as El Salvador's president.

A Nobel Prize Winner

In 1949, another international student came to New York for two years with his wife, Sonia, and his little daughter, Zviva. Years later, Shimon Peres was awarded the Nobel Peace Prize. In his autobiography, *Battling for Peace*, he writes about his time in New York and Boston, saying, "It was a formulative period both of my life and of my intellectual and political development. . . . Every corner of that great country presents fascinating information and insights for the curious observer. I was immediately swept up by the originality, ingenuity, and boundless enthusiasm of the people, especially the young." While Peres doesn't give a great number of details or stories about his time in the U.S., he draws an interesting characterization of America, saying, "Despite all the materialism in American society, it is not the dollar that is the strong underpinning of that society but the Bible, both the New Testament and the Old. By the same token, the basis of the special relationship that developed between the United States and Israel was not a common enemy but rather common values."

From his words and tone, you note that Peres developed strong friendships while in the United States. While firmly holding to his Jewish faith, he expresses openness to a spiritual dialogue with Christians. Some of these impressions were formed early in his time abroad.

The First Modern Woman Muslim Leader

In *Daughter of Destiny*, Benazir Bhutto writes about her education at Harvard-Radcliffe. Her father, Zufikar Al Bhutto, was the Prime Minister of Pakistan. In 1988, nine years after his execution, Benazir became the first woman to lead a Muslim nation in modern times. Before Benazir went to college, her father gave her a beautiful copy of the Quran and told her, "You will see many things that surprise you in America and some that may shock you. But I know you have the ability to adapt. Above all you must study hard. Very few in Pakistan have the opportunity you now have, and you must take advantage of it. Never forget that the money it is costing to send you comes from the land, from the people who sweat and toil on those lands. You will owe a debt to them, a debt you can repay with God's blessing by using your education to better their lives." These words give insight into the motivation and pressures that international students face when coming to America.

She writes about her early days in college. " 'Pak-i-*stan*? Where's Pak-i-*stan*?' my new classmates asked me when I first arrived at Radcliffe.

"Pakistan is the largest Muslim country in the world," I replied, sounding like a handout from our embassy. "There are two wings of Pakistan, separated by India."

"Oh, India," came the relieved response. "You're next to India."

"I smarted every time I heard the reference to India, with whom we had had two bitter wars. Pakistan was supposed to be one of America's strongest allies. . . . The United States used our air bases in northern Pakistan for their U-2 reconnaissance flights, including the ill-fated flight of Gary Powers even in 1960. . . . Yet Americans seemed completely unaware of even the existence of my country."

Today, Benazir Bhutto takes her experiences from the land of Harvard into her everyday decisions and actions as she leads this Muslim nation.

Some Students Come With Christian Backgrounds

Not every international student comes to America without a Christian background. In fact, two African Christian leaders studied at Lincoln University in Oxford, Pennsylvania. Nnamdi Azikiwe was the founder of modern Nigerian nationalism and the first president of Nigeria (1963–1966). As a Lincoln student, Azikiwe became one of the most earnest recruiting agents for Lincoln in West Africa. One of his recruits was Kwame Nkrumah, who became the first prime minister and president of Ghana. As a student in the U.S., Nkrumah earned a Master of Science degree at the University of Pennsylvania and, in the same year, a Bachelor of Sacred Theology degree from Lincoln Seminary. During his summers at Lincoln, Nkrumah worked as a colporteur and research student of the religious practices among African-Americans. In 1942, he wrote, "Almost every one of my Sundays has been devoted to preaching either in Philadelphia, New York, or Washington." Horace Mann Bond, author of *Education for Freedom*, wrote about Nkrumah, "He was seeing life in the raw and sharing in the humble joys, defeats, and exaltations of the American Negro, his overseas cousin." Years later, Nkrumah became a leader in Ghana and guided his nation from colonial rule to independence. A major portion of his theological and religious training came from his years in the United States.

Hundreds of thousands of international students are studying in the United States. In five to twenty years, they will be the leaders of their nations. They *will* return home to make a difference. The question is, "Will they make a difference for Jesus Christ?" As they attend the university, these students face a marketplace of ideas. At the university, they formulate ideas about the world, their belief system, and values. Long ago, Marxist and communist leaders realized the power and potential they possessed to influence young university students, and worked diligently toward this end.

Abraham Lincoln said, "The philosophy of the classroom today will soon be the philosophy of the government and the nation tomorrow." The sixteenth President clearly observed a link between young minds and the direction of the nation. Many years later, Adolph Hitler agreed, saying, "Let me control the textbooks and the ideas postulated in the classroom, and I will control Germany."

Martin Luther said, "Schools rule the world."

Social changes for our world most often come from the universities and like-minded institutions. Chuck Colson says in *Against the Night*:

> Profound social changes often trace their origins not to sinister conspiracies but to the paneled libraries of genial philosophers or the study alcoves of the British Museum or the crowded cafes of our universities. *Powerful movements are rooted in the realm of ideas* (italics by authors).

These world leaders present an incredible mission field. Here's a brief list of past and present world leaders who have trained in our universities:

Belize: George C. Price, Prime Minister; St. Augustine Seminary, Mississippi

Cyprus: George Vasiliou, President; Harvard University

Ecuador: Sixto Duran, President; Columbia University, New York

Ireland: Mary Robinson, President; Harvard University

Israel: Benjamin Netanyahu, Prime Minister; Massachusetts Institute of Technology.

Ivory Coast: Alassone Ouattara, Prime Minister; University of Pennsylvania

Japan: Masako Owado, Princess; Harvard University

Jordan: Tahir al-Masri, Prime Minister; North Texas State University

Liberia: Charles Taylor, Leader NPFL rebels; Bentley

Mexico: Carlos Salinas, President; Harvard University

New Zealand: Geoffrey Palmer, Former Governor General; University of Chicago

Nicaragua: Violeta Barrios de Chamorro, President; Blackstone College

Philippines: Corazon Aquino, Former President; Mount St. Vincent College

Singapore: Goh Chok Tong, Prime Minister; Williams College

Sudan: John Garang, Leader SPLA rebels; Cornell

Sweden: Ingvar Carlsson, Prime Minister; Northwestern University

Taiwan: Lein Chan, Premier; University of Chicago

Taiwan: Lee Teng-hui, President; Iowa State, Cornell

Turkey: Tansu Ciller, Prime Minister; Yale

Virtually every continent and part of the world is represented, and this list is only a small sample of the leaders who were educated in the

United States. Many others are not top-level governmental leaders yet still have powerful influence over the industry, education, economics, science, politics, technology, agriculture, and faith of their countries. Several years ago, a Colorado family became friends with a Peruvian student. During his education in America, this family developed a close relationship, and, while the student attended religious functions, he never made a personal commitment to Jesus Christ. After completion of his studies, the young man returned home and eventually became the head of the Department of Education.

At the time, the government was suspicious of the motives of Wycliffe Bible Translators. They sent the head of the Department of Education to investigate Wycliffe and determine if the mission organization should stay in Peru or not. This man was overwhelmed by the love of the American family in Colorado as well as the loving attitude of Wycliffe personalities during his investigation. He was convinced the organization was a benefit to his people, should remain in Peru, and in his report recommended no further action. Today, Wycliffe's work of Bible translation in Peru is almost finished. The attitude of this Peruvian government official was shaped through a loving friendship outreach during his college days—from a family who selflessly shared Christ's love with him.

Mark Rentz from the American Language and Cultural Program in Arizona has studied more than 3,000 returning students who are now leaders in their countries. When these students were asked about the value of their experience in America, nearly all of the respondents said it was not their academic experience that they remember. Instead, the most valuable experience to them was their time with Americans and the opportunity to experience life in America. Relationship is key in the formulation of ideas. One can not divorce the emotion from the rationale.

Our World Isn't Far Removed

Twenty-four hour radio and television stations blast the news into our homes. When a disaster or breaking story happens, we turn on CNN and watch as events unfold across the globe. It's sometimes easy to turn away from a horrible disaster in another country or remove ourselves from the ongoing trauma in a distant location such as the Middle East. We rationalize, "Well, it's so far away."

Or, we feel helpless to do anything about the situation. "I'm only one person. How could I make a difference?" Well, we *can* make a difference in our world even if it is only one person at a time. We can accomplish this feat of love without ever leaving our homes. For example, Weiming Cao of China wrote of his appreciation for Dr. Jim and Nancy Katekaru. Jim, a retired professor from Cal-Poly Technical Institute, has a Ph.D. in chemistry. Now living in Honolulu while Nancy is battling cancer, they are working as staff members with International Students, Incorporated. Weiming writes, "I'm a visiting scholar, and this September my wife left and went back to China. I had to move out of the house where we lived, and Mr. and Mrs. Katekaru provided a house to me. When I lived with them, they told me much information about Christianity that makes sense to me and I made a decision to receive Jesus as my Savior. After that, I felt peaceful and happy. Thank God."

Admittedly, the world is a huge place. In the United States alone there are more than 250 million people, and the world has a population of almost six billion. It's easy to be overwhelmed by this mass of humanity.

But instead of feeling insignificant, let's consider the possibilities. Dr. Bill Bright, founder of Campus Crusade for Christ, says, "Every soul is equally precious in God's sight, but not every soul is equally strategic." Every individual who does not have a personal relationship with Jesus Christ is lost and bound for an eternity separated from love, from God. In our day-to-day activities, it's easy to lose that perspective for helping, that passion to help the lost people around us.

The Historic Approach for Overseas Missions

Traditionally the Church and individuals have trained for going to the world with the Good News about Jesus. Our view of missions is nearly always dominated by the picture of an individual or family being called to quit their job, pack their belongings, and move to another part of the world in order to minister to people in another culture. For people to make this commitment is a strategic and key part of God's plan. It is born out of the familiar passage in Matthew 28:19-20, "Therefore go and make disciples of all nations, baptizing them in the name of the Father and of the Son and of the Holy Spirit, and teaching them to obey everything I have commanded you." However, let's consider this historical approach in light of a constantly changing world, our place at the end of the twentieth century, and God's present plan.

Bible college graduates James and Mary trained in linguistics for a cross-cultural ministry. It wasn't easy, and it took them several years to raise enough prayer and financial support to move overseas to Papua New Guinea. Despite their excellent training, they were not prepared for the drastic change of lifestyle. After a few weeks, Mary couldn't stand their living situation, and they returned home. They've never been back. Sadly, for one reason or another, James and Mary's situation as overseas missionaries is fairly common.

Statistics show that over the last 100 years less than half of one percent of American and Canadian Christians have actually heard that call to international missions and gone out to work overseas. As the last generation of career missionaries returns home, they are not being replaced by a flow of new recruits.

One missionary agency reported to ISI that it costs over $90,000 a year for a foreign missionary couple to live and work in Japan. After these new missionaries arrive in Japan, it will take them two years of language study before they will be able to fluently communicate about their faith in Jesus Christ and help someone to make a personal spiritual commitment to Christ as Lord and Savior.

A Blessing to the Nations

In Genesis 12, God gave a blessing to Abraham, the father of the Jewish people. He said, "I will make you into a great nation and I will bless you; I will make your name great, and you will be a blessing. I will bless those who bless you, and whoever curses you I will curse; and all peoples on earth will be blessed through you" (Genesis 12:2-3). Through the spiritual seed of Abraham, the nations will be blessed as we follow God's promise and plan. We obediently accomplish his blessing in two ways:

1. Going to the nations.
2. Ministering to individuals from the nations who come to us.

For centuries, historic missions has dealt with the first method. Yet missions as a sending opportunity is changing. There are now at least four approaches to missions:

1. *The apostolic missions approach* in which missionaries are called, ordained, experienced, and trained. Appropriately, they are still going to areas of the world where there is no Church. Outsiders, through Christ's love, minister, help others to know Christ, plant churches, and disciple.

2. *The assistance approach* to indigenous ministries. This approach is more recent. Missionaries from our nation are resourced, trained, and called to come alongside indigenous laborers who need their assistance.

3. Another approach is to *resource and support indigenous missionaries*, nationals whom God has raised up for ministry. Recently the first convocation of mission agencies supporting indigenous workers was held at the Billy Graham Center at Wheaton College. Fifty-four agencies were represented!

4. *Get out of the way*. Some parts of our world that have been developing spiritually are now at a point where they can carry their own load in the missionary enterprise. South Korea, for example, is a nation that is ministering to the rest of the world through their own gifted individuals and have organizations to support them.

Besides these approaches to missions, the *short-term missions movement* is growing with enormous momentum. A major church in Minnesota is a prime example of this explosive growth. Their goal is to have 2,000 short-term missionaries involved by the year 2000. Over 1,100 have participated to date. This effort accomplishes some dramatic results in the local church:

1. Personal involvement by their people in missions.
2. Blessings to the people to whom they minister overseas.
3. Revitalization of the heart and approach of missions.
4. Future support for missions throughout the local body.

The World Is at Our Door

While it has always been God's plan for the Church to go to the world, this strategy is only half of God's equation for reaching the people who don't have a personal relationship with Christ. Over the centuries, the Church has missed or nearly missed an equally significant part of God's plan—reaching the world that God brings to the Church. The New Testament book of Acts records in its early pages how men and women were gathered together from around the world. In Jerusalem, these people heard the Gospel of Jesus Christ, accepted it, and returned to their countries as ambassadors for God.

Today history repeats itself in the U.S., where over 500,000 of the world's best, brightest, and/or privileged students from every nation are within minutes of a local church. Such a representative gathering is unparalleled in human history. These students are attending America's institutions of higher learning. Their present quest is not for land or gold but for the prestige of an American education or a grasp of new Western technologies. These future leaders will return to their societies with the competitive skills for the geo-economic race into the future.

Each year over 120,000 new international students and scholars begin a four-year sojourn in American universities and other institutions of higher learning. While these students come to America with specific goals and plans, most of them are unaware of a personal divine plan from God. As caring and committed Christians come across their paths and offer friendship in Him, they can learn about the greatest friend of all—Jesus Christ.

Immersed in a new culture and away from family and friends, these international students are often lonely. They often feel out of place, lost, and anxious about understanding new people and a new situation. Simple tasks can be bewildering for the international student—as they would be to us if we were overseas for a period of time—such as how to locate housing or banking, or the difference between a grocery store, drugstore, specialty shops, and a department store. When these internationals face these challenges alone, daily life can become extremely discouraging to them.

Several years ago, one of our staff attended a college president's reception for incoming international students at a California university. The president tried a creative idea. He had two graduating seniors tell about their experience in the U.S. during the last few years. After the first senior spoke, it was an idea he regretted.

A Middle Eastern student stood stiffly behind the podium and began, "I have been in America for four years, and these have been the most lonely years of my life. When I walk down a hallway and an American says with a smile, 'Hi, how are you doing?' I stop and try to tell them how I am doing. Instead, they just keep on walking and don't really care about my answer."

The heart of the staff member sank at the thought of this lasting impression on an international visitor who was about to return to his homeland. Our ministry, International Students, Incorporated, notes that this student's story is all too commonplace. Statistics prove that among the international students who study in the U.S., historically 70 percent have never been invited to an American home during their stay. More than 85 percent are never invited to an American church or have any meaningful contact with genuine Christians during an average stay of four years.

Still there is good news from these statistics. These students feel a tremendous need for relationship. They are open to anyone who will stretch out their hand and say, "I'll be your friend." We can change these statistics—one lonely student at a time—each of us can be that friend.

Peling, from China, said after coming to the United States to study, "In my country, I had friends but no freedom. Here, I had much freedom but no friends." As you note her statement you can sense the desperation in her voice. Then Peling climaxed this cry from the wilderness with, "Then I met friends at ISI and through them met the greatest Friend of all, Jesus Christ."

During the 1920s, Yosuki Matsuoki, from Japan, came to Portland, Oregon, and studied at the university. While in the U.S., Matsuoki felt poorly treated. He returned home hateful and embittered about America. Over time, he rose through the ranks of power. Finally he got his revenge on the American people when he assisted in the planning and execution of the Japanese attack on Pearl Harbor.

The course of history might have been different during the 1940s if the lonely student Matsuoki had been befriended by loving Christians twenty years earlier.

Mengistu Mariam, from Ethiopia, arrived at Aberdeen, Maryland, in the 1950s for military training. He soon became embittered and resentful as a result of the way he was treated by Americans. Over time, he too rose to a position of power, and in 1974 was a key figure in the coup against King Haile Selassie. Mariam established a Marxist government and began a relentless campaign to root out what he called "alien religion" in Ethiopia, even though Christianity originated in the Middle East. In an address to the nation, Mariam called missionaries the number one source of imperialist infiltration in the past. Shortly after the speech, he expelled all missionaries and made it impossible for anyone who attempted to evangelize to continue their work. He also confiscated a $15 million missionary radio station and began to broadcast Marxist propaganda. Churches were closed, and believers in Jesus Christ fell under intense religious persecution, including frequent imprisonment. The key leader in this effort was one international student who had a bad experience in the "land of the free."

In stark contrast is the experience of Bakht Singh, a Sikh man who came from northern India to study engineering in Canada. This young Indian began his studies like any other foreign student, but a Christian couple reached out to Bakht in friendship and love. They gave him a Bible and encouraged him to meet other Christians. Through their friendship, Bakht accepted Christ. The couple also taught him the Scriptures. Later he returned to India not only as an engineer but as a preacher and evangelist. As a result of his faithful work for Christ, over 700 churches have been established in India, Pakistan, Sri Lanka, and Nepal.

Time magazine attests to the exploding opportunities to shape future leaders at American universities. In an April 13, 1992 article, Jim Smolowe says, "American universities and colleges are the envy of the world. For all their abiding troubles, this country's 3,500 institutions were flooded with 407,530 foreign students (a number up nearly 150,000 in six years with enrollment at 554,000 in 1997) from 193 different countries last year. Asia led the way with 40,000 from the Peoples Republic of China, and 36,610 from Japan, followed by India and Canada." In fact, international students are capturing a large proportionate share of the Ph.D.s awarded annually in the United States.

Beverly Watkins, in the *Chronicle of Higher Education*, stated, "The U.S. educates more foreign students than any other country in the world. Nearly one-third of all students worldwide who study abroad enroll at U.S. institutions." Nearly 75 percent of these students and scholars use funds from family or other non-U.S. resources for their primary means of financial support during their studies, says Richard Krasno with the Institute of International Education. This fact points out that these students come from the upper levels of their society. Traditional missionaries would rarely meet or impact these people, but near our homes, we can meet, interact with, and serve these future leaders. These young people are incredibly sensitive, kind, and appreciative. They don't know that they are future leaders. Dressed in running shoes, jeans, and open-collar shirts, they are respectful, yet personally searching for a friend—away from their traditional peer pressure, family pressure, political pressure, and religious pressure. In the midst of their pilgrimage is a search for truth, and we have the honor of loving each one of them for Christ's sake.

The 10/40 Window

In the last few years, a number of mission agencies have highlighted the need for Christ in a small targeted area of the world called the 10/40 window. This is a geographical belt confined between the tenth and fortieth degree parallel stretching from northwest Africa to across the eastern islands of the Philippines. The belt represents the resident majority of the unreached people groups in the world—people who have never had a chance to hear about Jesus Christ. Research shows that 97 percent of the people who live in the least-evangelized countries are located in the 62 countries that compose the 10/40 window. This geographic location is of particular interest because of the 1,746 unreached people groups there. Of the international students from countries closed or less than accessible to the Gospel of Jesus Christ, over 50 percent are from this 10/40 window. Yet their future leaders and executives are *here*.

In God's plan, he has brought these leaders to our door. In many cases, it is difficult or impossible for traditional missionaries to enter these nations. Nearly 37,000,000 Christians are known to have been praying for the people of the 10/40 window, and 607 groups have made prayer journeys to the "100 Gateway Cities" of those nations, with 143,447 churches involved. Prayer is vital, as is shown by these statistics compiled by Beverly Peques of the Christian Information Network in Colorado Springs, Colorado. It's important to have creative ideas for reaching these nations in person. Yet many future and current leaders of these countries aren't presently in their countries. They are studying in our universities and are right on your doorstep.

As the Church is mobilized to "go" to this region, *it is entirely possible that we will overlook the fact the future leaders of the 10/40 window are here now*. These leaders are easily reached with the Good News about Jesus through friendship and love. This important opportunity must not be overlooked by the 10/40 window strategists. It is perhaps the most practical and strategic way for the average American to have a long-term impact on the unreached people of our world. Few American Christians will go to live in the 10/40 window countries, yet the majority of these Americans live within a few minutes of a 10/40 window student.

Our Journey Ahead

In the following pages, we will address some of the misconceptions and fears about working with international students. Developing a friendship with internationals isn't complicated or frightening. We will show you how to easily entertain them in your home, and give ideas about how to converse with them and develop a friendship. Then, with simple steps, we will show you how to respectfully present the claims of Christ to an international student and help the individual grow in his or her Christian faith. Finally, we'll share tips from our combined years of ministry experience regarding how to help these international friends when they return to their homelands. Also, the book will address some of the many benefits for the local church, and how you can befriend or mentor a future leader and join a national movement. The book will mix the practical with motivational stories so you will become excited about the possibilities—no matter what your age or Christian experience.

Apply What You've Learned

The chapters within this book are more than simply motivational. Our desire and prayer is that you will be challenged to grow in your Christian life and touch your world for Christ. Each chapter will conclude with several ready-to-apply suggestions, which are developed from its contents.

1. *Consider the world.* In our day-to-day activities with family and friends, it's easy to think our influence is limited. You will see that it is not. Begin in prayer to ask about your own role in influencing your world. Commit to spending time each day praying about how you can apply the material on these pages to your own life.

2. *Find a map of the world.* The average American has a limited understanding of geography. Where is Zimbabwe? Can you locate Taiwan on a map, or Argentina? At your local office supply or bookstore, purchase a world map and post it where you'll see it every day. Use the map as a tool not only to learn about the locations of different countries but also as a prayer device. Specifically pray for God to move in the hearts of international students and to use your life to influence theirs for good.

3. *Begin to pray for the unreached peoples of the 10/40 window.* Send for the "Praying Through the Window" materials designed to inform you about the unreached people groups of the world. Specifically ask for the "International Student 10/40 Window Brochure" (see Appendix A for ordering instructions). Begin to pray that God will lead you to a relationship with a potential future 10/40 window leader who is studying on a campus in your area.

TWO

Understanding Students and Meeting Their Needs

"I can do everything through him who gives me strength."

Philippians 4:13

"For it is God who works in you to will and to act according to his good purpose."

Philippians 2:13

Every few months, Joe and Mary heard their pastor announce an opportunity to help international students in their town. "It's friendship, plain and simple," the pastor would say with a smile. "But it could change lives significantly. Give Gary a call if you're interested. . . ." Joe and Mary typically thought about something else the minute they heard the word "international." After all, they had never been out of the country or even traveled around the U.S. much. What would they have in common with an international student? Could they even begin a conversation? What if the student doesn't speak English? What if he or she doesn't like our food? And in their small apartment, they certainly didn't have room for an international student to live with them.

This young couple holds many of the common misconceptions people often have toward a friendship with international students. Friendship is just what it means—friendship. This relationship begins small and can grow to various depths and commitment levels. Here are five things that friendship with an international does *not* involve:

1. The student does not live in your home. While some people choose to be a host family and ask a student to live with them, scores of thousands have chosen to be what we call "friendship partners." As a friendship partner, they get together once or twice a month to build a relationship with the student and talk on the phone or communicate through e-mail messages.

2. It does not require a financial commitment. In fact, you are encouraged not to become involved in any financial matters with an international student. It's friendship, not sponsorship.

3. It does not require legal sponsorship. These students are already here in the U.S. and have housing on their particular university setting, or their own apartment or house. They are responsible for their own legal status within the country and the resulting obligations. Not only is it not your responsibility, we do not encourage such a relationship.

4. It does not require that you speak a foreign language or that you be an expert about the particular country of the student. Students studying in our universities must pass the Test of English Fluency (TOEFL) with a good proficiency in the language before they can be accepted into our higher learning institutions.

5. It does not involve a major alteration or adjustment to your lifestyle! Many people feel like they must go to great lengths and set up special events or impressive activities for their international students. Students aren't interested in these special events or elaborate activities. Instead, they want to see the inside of an American home and have the opportunity to observe the everyday life of an American family. These students are happy to join any family activity and are thrilled to be included.

The Tables Are Turned

For a few moments, consider all the typical fears and challenges for an overseas missionary. These aspects are reversed in a friendship outreach to international students. Most missionaries face the challenges of raising financial support, learning another language, adjusting to a completely different culture, separation from family and friends, and often fear of failure and rejection.

Conversely, as previously stated, when we become friendship partners to international students in our country, the tables are turned. It is the student who is facing all of the awkward and stressful challenges of adapting to our culture, language, and environment.

Permit this understanding of the international student to alleviate your fears. You are in a position of loving strength. As you come alongside your new international friends, they view you as the expert. You are someone they can trust and who can help them make their way in this new and unfamiliar country. You have an advantage in this area over any overseas missionary. You have the opportunity to minister to the foreign student in your own country! In addition, the student senses that he or she really desires you and your friendship.

Walk in Another Person's Shoes

Let's take an imaginary trip to another country for a few minutes. Let's say you have an intense interest in Near Eastern archaeology and you decide to study for a semester in Egypt. After traveling for thirty hours to get to the country, you step off the plane and a blast of heat hits you in the face. The heat seems to hang in the air with an intensity you've never felt before. With great difficulty, in the midst of a dry sauna, you locate your bags and shuffle through customs. With some effort, you manage to tell a cab driver that you'd like to go to the university.

The cab driver knows you are a foreigner and takes you the "long" route, which involves an extra thirty minutes of driving and a much larger fare. When you finally reach the university, nothing is open because you've arrived on a holy day. So the driver takes you to a nearby hotel.

Before coming to Egypt, you had been studying Arabic and thought you were fluent. At least you made good grades in your Arabic classes, but now that you are in Egypt, everyone talks so fast and seems to think *you* have a strong accent. At the restaurant in the hotel, you try to find something "normal" to eat but everything looks different and you wonder where to begin. Exhausted from your travels, you drop into bed. At 5:00 A.M. you are startled awake by blaring horns that call people to prayer. You begin to wonder: "Will I ever like it here? Can I understand the Egyptian ways of life?"

International students, including those who are well-respected leaders in their own country, arrive in the United States with the same fears and concerns. The simplest tasks become enormously complicated, and many face plans that fall apart or situations that are unexpected.

One evening as an ISI family sat down to dinner, the conversation around the table was broken by the ring of the telephone.

"Hello, is Bob there?" came the Hispanic-sounding voice on the phone.

"Yes, this is Bob. How can I help you?"

"I am Euginio Ponce from Peru and I heard you speak at the university orientation this morning about your program for American friends. I went to my host family where the university has set up for me to live. But when I got there they say they change their mind. I have no where to go."

"And where are you now, Euginio?" Bob asks.

"I have my suitcases and I am in a pay phone booth downtown."

Within half an hour, Euginio was in Bob's home. Soon "Coco," as he was called, became a part of the family. Eventually, he made a personal commitment to Jesus Christ.

Euginio's experience with host families is not uncommon. Most students have no one to meet them at the airport when they arrive in America, or no one to help them find the campus. Oftentimes, their best laid plans fall apart. If you are available to step into these situations at the student's time of need, you will make a lifetime friend.

Like another student, Pam Cheng, said: "When you first come to America, it is very confusing. The first thing we face is loneliness. We need to have a friend to talk with who can explain things to us. It is very different. We need to know how to open a bank account, how to get around town. We need to know what bus to take and how to get tickets for the train. Many times we don't know where to shop and what is the difference between grocery store and department store and what in the world is K-Mart!"

Students like Euginio and Pam are typical in their experience and the first months of adjustment. These first few weeks in America bring one bewildering experience after another. Your friendship outreach may begin with nothing more than being there to meet needs. Activities and time spent picking up your students at the airport, helping them get settled, showing them around town, and helping them with English will afford you opportunity for deep impact on their lives. It's an experience that for overseas missionaries takes months or even years to develop.

A Different Arrival

Jiang recently arrived in the U.S. from China and was learning his way around the university and struggling with his accounting classes. Jiang had a wife and a one-year-old son who would remain in Beijing for the time Jiang was in the U.S. His mother, who was in poor health, was also living in Beijing. Because of his upbringing and education in China, Jiang was suspicious about Christianity, but he was willing to have American Christian friends.

Through a friendship program at their local church and in cooperation with the local university, Alan and Jan Carlson became interested in an international friendship. Alan is a CPA and Jan is a homemaker. Because Jiang is studying for a business degree, he was matched with the Carlson family. They have been Christians for about six years. They have a six-year-old daughter and an eight-year-old son, and Jan's father, who is in poor health, lives with them.

First, the Carlsons invited Jiang to their home for dinner. There were no opportunities prior to the meal to discuss spiritual matters. Before they ate, Alan prayed and thanked God for their meal. Jiang politely joined the prayer time and then said, "The only person that I know who believed in God was my aunt in Shanghai. She also prayed before her meals." The Carlsons wanted to carry on a spiritual discussion with Jiang, but they struggled to know where to begin. Surprisingly, Jiang opened the discussion without much effort. This is commonplace, since international students don't carry a stigma regarding discussion of religion like most Americans do. The Carlsons know that as they love Christ other opportunities to share will come about in the natural course of the friendship. In the meantime, they will enjoy Jiang as a person and include him on family outings such as a picnic or a shopping trip. He is happy to go whenever invited and his intense study schedule allows.

The Carlsons and Jiang are in the early stages of a friendship. Alan and Jan are simply helping Jiang with some of his basic relational needs, and it doesn't take any special skill to accomplish these tasks. Just being a friend for Christ's sake is all that is required.

Practical Needs You Can Meet

Anything new is challenging. You may feel inadequate or afraid of a new relationship with an international student. Let's examine some of the needs of this person and how you can meet them in simple ways:

Physical Needs: International students will often face tremendous physical needs during their first weeks in the United States. Arrival in the U.S. is often the end of a grueling cross-country race of preparation, packing, saying goodbye to family and friends, and hours of sleepless travel before reaching their final destination.

As mentioned earlier, students typically arrive with no one to greet them at the airport, and they are unsure of how to locate their campus and housing on their own. An American family or friend who awaits them with a smile and an offer of temporary lodging and a comfortable bed is a gift that can seldom be outdone. There is perhaps no greater avenue for bonding with your new friend than to meet them as they step off the plane and to bring them to your home. You will be remembered forever.

Another very practical way to meet physical needs is to provide for household items for students as they set up their new place of residence. In Portland, Oregon, Christians throughout the year collect couches, dressers, beds, pots and pans, and all sorts of household goods and store them for the new school year. Each fall new international students are given passes to the Portland "Garage Giveaway" put on by the Christian churches of Greater Portland and International Students, Incorporated. Through this give-away students see a tangible expression of God's love for them as they set up their homes.

Another great physical need for students is a craving for food that is familiar. Students love to share their culture and are often thrilled to take over your kitchen and prepare some food for you and your family from his or her country. You might research grocery stores that specialize in ethnic foods not common in American grocery stores. The Chinese students in Colorado Springs used to drive to a Chinese grocer in Denver, an hour away, every couple of weeks in order to buy ingredients for their ethnic cooking.

A student may be athletic, or even a soccer star in his home country.

There is probably an exercise facility on his campus that he could use at little or no cost. But he may need your guidance and help to find it, understand how to use the lockers and the system for use of towels. You could work out with the student and develop your friendship together in play as well as conversation.

Talk with the student about security. Many countries have a strong military presence, and the police are greatly feared. You could let students know that they can trust the police on their campus or in their community. Also encourage them not to go out alone at night and also to lock the doors to their rooms and dwellings.

Mental Needs: These new arrivals in the United States often speak a limited amount of English. You can help them practice their skills. Their vocabulary may be extremely limited when it comes to colloquial sayings or idioms, so think about these aspects when talking with them. Imagine some of the images that are conjured up in the minds of students as they interpret some of our idioms literally. For instance, what might the student think when they hear that some of us stay after church just to "shoot the breeze." Or how about hearing that the registrar at the school "jumped the gun" in telling him that he was definitely enrolled in the morning accounting class. Or what about the expression "It's raining cats and dogs?"

There is perhaps no easier way to spend time ministering to an international student than to come alongside him as a conversational English partner and to help him gain a better command of our language.

Also understand that their studies are the top priority, so don't make too many demands on their time. Many friendship partners have offered to assist students by reading their papers before they submit them to their professors, and make suggestions on grammar or presentation. Students often appreciate this because their studies are so vitally important to them.

Many of these students are already brilliant in their particular field of expertise. Talk with them about world events and their views and perspectives on life in general. Later on we will detail specific topics of conversation, but the key is to let the students express themselves and to be interested in their needs. For example, make sure they know it's okay to talk with their professor. Many students are from cultures where the teacher is the ultimate authority and out of respect is not to be questioned or challenged. Students need to know the freedom they have in our Western system of learning.

Social Needs: Students will naturally be attracted to others from their own country. You can help them develop new friendships outside this sphere of people who speak their native language. Introduce them to your Christian friends. A word of caution is necessary about touching and overfriendliness—particularly with the opposite sex. Be sensitive to different cultural expectations. For example, Asians are unaccustomed to touching, especially from the opposite sex. In friendly religious contexts, we sometimes are accustomed to hugging. Be aware that such touching may not be appropriate or may be misinterpreted by the international.

Emotional Needs: How do you handle new things in your life? Think about change and how you adapt to it. Some do it easily, but some have great difficulty. Cultural changes are also difficult. The international student feels like there is so much to learn about the American way of life. You can help students develop an attitude of trust where they can talk about their feelings and emotional difficulties. One of the commonplace reactions to a new culture is to pull into your shell like a turtle. It's lonely inside that shell, and you can help the student face his or her fears and overcome them.

Spiritual Needs: While spiritual concerns are a key motivation for us to interact with an international student, make sure it's not your single focus and only motivation. Students sense when they are merely a target for evangelism. They also know when you are sincere and genuine toward them with "no strings attached." Your first priority should be reaching out to the student's needs and from there developing a basis to talk about spiritual matters. In this sense it's no different than reaching out to a neighbor or a business associate.

Initially you will not know the international's attitude about religion or spirituality. Take the time to ask about their experiences. He or she will probably be willing to talk about the topic but make sure you avoid arguments or heated discussions. You will find that many African Muslims attended missionary schools for their education. Some Chinese, who generally are atheists, have attended Baptist high schools. This often opens the door to discuss their views on the Christian faith.

It is appropriate to invite your international friend to attend a church service, wedding, funeral, or baptism. You can free the student from pressure by inviting him to come simply as an observer. Many students believe that it is American to be a Christian.

Mohammed flew into the San Francisco airport and was met by Frank Currie, an ISI staff member who at the time was working at UC Berkeley. As they made their way back through town, traffic to the Bay Bridge was detoured onto the city streets of the North Beach District, notorious for its live strip joints, pornography shops, and illicit sexual opportunity.

The rapid get-to-know-you conversation screeched to a halt as Mohammed sat in wonder at the flashing neon signs announcing seemingly every sin in the Bible on one city block. Billboards of half-naked women towered over entrances to dark night clubs, each with a barker in front beckoning passersby to indulge in the show inside.

Mohammed looked at Frank in shock and said, "I do not understand, why do Christians have this kind of place. My God Allah would never allow this in my country. I think Islam is better than Christianity."

For the remainder of the trip, Frank explained the difference between cultural Christian roots in America and genuine Christianity. Mohammed's beliefs and preconceived notions of America are common to many students. They don't understand that all Americans are not Christians. When the cultural situation is reversed, we tend to draw the same conclusions: i.e., that a Latin American is Roman Catholic; a person from Saudi Arabia is Muslim; a person from Thailand is a Buddhist, etc. Talk with the international about how our culture is distinct from our faith. Do not be discouraged. The ever-increasing darkness of our culture allows us as Christians to stand out in stark contrast to what students see in the non-Christian part of our culture.

Many students, especially Asians, feel that a balanced life indicates a successful society. Therefore, they are very interested in our spiritual life because they feel that it has had a major contribution in our success.

Local Acclimation Needs: Every international faces thousands of questions, most of which are usually easy for you to answer. Here are seven practical ways you can help someone:

1. Show the student around the area. Explain how he can use the public transportation system (you may first have to learn yourself if you haven't used it). Show him how to use a parking meter and a pay phone. These devices are probably different in his country.

2. Show him where to find a public rest room when he is away from his residence. Explain that rest rooms are usually available in department stores, restaurants, hotels, etc. Tell him it is safe to drink the water.

3. Help him set up a bank account and/or a telephone service. Explain how to use a toll-free 800 number, and the charges involved with using a 900 number.

4. Help him shop in a grocery store. Help him locate foods and seasonings from his country. Help him select a particular store for shopping. Explain the many possibilities. Explain how to use coupons from the newspaper. One international student came home from the grocery store with a can of Crisco. She thought it was chicken because chicken was pictured on the label.

5. Teach the student about tipping in restaurants and other places.

6. Explain the difference between a Wal-Mart store and a Neiman Marcus. Introduce students to the concept of buying furniture or used items through newspaper ads or at a garage sale. Give them pointers about when to shop—seasonal sales, year-end sales, etc.

7. If you are familiar with how to use the Internet, show your student how to use it.

Other practical tips for the student are included in a resource called *How to Survive in the U.S.*, from International Students, Incorporated. (See Appendix A.)

Meeting the Children's Needs: As an American, you have a lot of internal information about what is proper and what is not. If the international student has children, you can assist him, her, or the family in another range of needs:

1. Help the parents understand how to dress their children for school. They may come from a situation where children wear uniforms, and they need to know the public school system here doesn't require uniforms. As you assist them with these matters, their children will be able to merge into the American schools and not be the subject of laughter or embarrassment. Help parents feel at ease, knowing that children adjust to culture and language far more quickly than adults. They will often help their parents with language because they learn it so rapidly.

2. Explain the necessity of parents' involvement with their children's education. Schoolteachers are busy with a large number of students. Parents need to attend school meetings and express their willingness to get involved with their child. Explain that the teacher will not initiate such contact unless a student is having a problem, and by then it's usually too late for simple involvement; it's appropriate to schedule an appointment with the teacher to introduce the family's situation to him or her.

3. Help internationals understand the importance of their children's friendships, but also to be aware of their children's friends and get to know who they are.

4. Help them understand the advantages and disadvantages of television. Help them to achieve a balance with their children between healthy TV programming and inappropriate viewing as well as the danger of overexposure.

5. Take the international students and their children to the local public library. Show them how to use the card catalog (often computerized), then give them a brief tour of the library. Unless shown how, they may hesitate to ask questions at the reference desk or other places of assistance.

6. Help them learn about the inexpensive forms of entertainment available in the region. Show them the weekend edition of the local newspaper for ideas and possibilities for getting out and learning about the area.

Language Needs: You can help international students learn to speak better English and also to understand what's going on around them. It doesn't take any special language training to meet this need. Most of the time, it involves simply listening to the international and being available to help. Jeff went to lunch with his international friend, Abdul. The student wanted to buy lunch for his American friend and thought of the word "hospitality" when he said, "Let me hospitalize you." With patience and love, Jeff explained how to use the word "hospitality." What embarrassed Abdul was not this single use of the word but the fact that he had used the phrase on many occasions, and no one had taken the time to correct him.

The English speaker can also make language errors as well as the international. For example, Thelma was cooking and couldn't open a jar of tomato sauce. She asked her student, Roberto, from Mexico, to help. With ease, Roberto twisted open the jar. Thelma smiled and said, "Thank you. You are very macho." Instead of a smile, Roberto was horrified at the words and said, "No! No!" Later Thelma learned that in his part of Mexico, "macho" is used when referring to a man who sleeps with many women.

A Key to Meeting Needs

Awareness and sensitivity are two words that are crucial with internationals. Ask God how he wants you to be involved in their lives. These students are scattered throughout the United States, and some of them are on your doorstep.

The Russian Hockey Team was staying at the Broadmoor Hotel in Colorado Springs. A staff worker from International Students, Incorporated learned about these players and took a box of Russian Bibles to the hotel. He set the Bibles outside their hotel rooms. Later when he returned, all of the Bibles were gone. Look for opportunities in your neighborhood. Either students live nearby, or you'll meet them shopping in your grocery store.

Apply What You've Learned

1. Examine your fears about meeting people from other nations. What concerns come to mind? How can you face these concerns and begin to overcome them? Feel free to ask an international student to help you.

2. How can you increase your sensitivity and awareness of internationals who cross your path? Ask God to open your eyes to new opportunities for ministry and ways you can meet their needs.

3. Close your eyes and pretend you have just stepped off the airplane in China. You will not return to the U.S. for four to six years. Make a list of the needs you feel during your first week or month away from home. What emotions run through your heart and mind? Take your list and ask yourself what ministry programs you could build to meet the needs of international students in similar situations.

THREE

Felt Called But Didn't Go

"I planted the seed, Apollos watered it, but God made it grow. So neither he who plants nor he who waters is anything, but only God, who makes things grow."

1 Corinthians 3:6–7

Sometimes Judy felt overwhelmed with guilt. These strong feelings swelled whenever a missionary spoke at her church or the pastor talked about having a vision for the world. Each year when commitment Sunday rolled around, and people stood and committed their lives to world evangelism, Judy made sure she skipped out.

Every time Judy's thoughts or attention turned to overseas or to international matters, she flashed back to her childhood. As a young girl, Judy attended a series of evangelistic meetings. On the final night, the evangelist urged people to walk to the altar and give their lives to world evangelism. At eight years old, Judy felt caught up in the emotion of the evening. Her best friend, Betsy, stood and walked down the aisle. Under obvious peer pressure, Judy followed her friend to the front and dedicated her life to overseas missions. Her parents were particularly proud of her decision, but Judy experiences regular waves of guilt because her life took a different direction. During her final year of college, she met a godly man who was planning a career in business. Robert and Judy married after college, settled down in their community, and had three children. Judy has never traveled outside of the continental United States. To make matters worse, Judy has kept in touch with Betsy, who went into career missions in Africa. Each month, in fact, she gets reports and letters from Betsy about her significant ministry.

"The Lord called me," Judy told a visiting missionary, "but I never followed through on my call."

While some readers may scoff at Judy's feelings of guilt, there are people like her scattered throughout the church in this country. These individuals feel they've let God down because they don't work in full-time Christian service or because they are not missionaries overseas.

While there are those who are truly called to overseas missionary service, people like Judy may need to realize that the "go" of the Great Commission can be fulfilled in ways other than a career in missions.

Too often we miss the fact that the "go" means to go to people. Most of us think it means to go to another country. In fact, the "go" of the Great Commission may entail going no farther than the local university, where the nations of the world are already gathered. Many do not realize that dreams and desires for overseas ministry can be fulfilled without ever boarding a plane.

Following the Call to Go by Staying

At age seventy, Ethel Hatfield became a Christian. She felt grateful for her salvation and wanted to give the rest of her life in service to Christ. When she told the Sunday school director about her willingness to help, he said, "It's too bad, but we don't have a place for you in our program." Not easily discouraged, Ethel asked the Lord for opportunities.

One day while working in the flower garden in her front yard, a Chinese student stopped by and visited with her. He was on his way to the nearby university campus. Ethel invited the student inside for coffee. As days and weeks passed, their friendship grew. Eventually they began to study the Scriptures together, and the student invited other Chinese friends. Soon they were all involved in regular Bible study.

Two years later, Ethel died. At her funeral, seventy Chinese students stood at attention. Ethel Hatfield knew the meaning of missions. She was a missionary in the truest sense of the word . . . without ever leaving home.

God's Unique Answer to Missionary Prayer

David and Susan lived in a small town in the Midwest only blocks from their local college. Both David and Susan had a rich background in ministry. As a student, Susan had been involved in InterVarsity Christian Fellowship at Purdue. Though David and Susan didn't know each other at the time, both attended Urbana '79 and came away with a deep burden for world missions. Individually they prayed over the years, then as a couple after they met and married, for God to open a door of direction for them to go overseas. Though they prayed consistently, no doors opened.

In 1992, they both felt an overwhelming burden for China. Often they would drive past student housing at the college and see the Chinese house identified by Chinese characters on the front. They sensed the Lord wanting them to reach out to the Chinese on campus.

"During missions emphasis at church," says Susan, "the associate pastor of Bear Valley Church from Denver spoke about target ministries. At one point he highlighted the importance of being aware of international students in our midst and what a strategic mission field they are for us to reach. He said, 'Many of these students will be future leaders of the world when they return home.' At these words, suddenly these light bulbs were going off in my mind, and I knew that God was speaking to my heart. I really began to seriously pray about this vision.

"It was shortly after that weekend as I was parking my van in front of the house that God showed me. We never see international students walk by our home . . . never. But as I pulled up there were seven Asian students walking right by my house. I have no idea where they were going because we are not on the normal route students take to school. Before I could even get out of the car I heard very clearly from the Lord, 'You need to reach out to these internationals now. You need to go to the college and get names of students and invite them to your home.' And that's just what I did.

"That same day, I went to the campus and got the names of seven Chinese students from mainland China. We sent invitations to them to come to our home, and three of the seven accepted our invitation. That night began a ministry of hospitality. We had them back to our home numerous times for dinner, and took trips together to Chinatown in Chicago. Soon God blessed our relationships to the point where some began to study the Scripture with us on a regular basis.

"To our surprise, later in the year we found that we had gained a reputation among students on the campus. In our first meeting, students would often say, 'Oh, so you are David and Susan! I've heard many good things about you.'

"One day a Chinese scholar, a visiting professor of English, was on his way back from the library and my kids were out playing. I looked out the window to check on my kids and here is this Chinese man talking to my children. So I watched, thinking, *This is interesting; I'm sure he won't talk to them very long*. But the conversation kept going and going. So I thought to myself, *I'm going to go see who this fella is*. So I struck up a conversation with him and learned he had just been in the United States a month and was incredibly homesick. He shared how he was really suffering, having left his wife and son back in China. The culture shock was so great and he said he felt incredibly lonely. 'I decided,' the scholar said, 'instead of becoming depressed, that I would go and talk to children because they are not threatening and they are so accepting and will talk with me. This helps my loneliness.'

"We invited him to dinner and over the next nine months we became close friends. He told some friends of ours before he returned to China, 'I want to be a Christian, please pray for me. I am going back to China and I will miss the Christians. I love being with the Christians.'"

During an evangelistic potluck for twenty students at David and Susan's home, this once lonely professor's heart was receptive to the Gospel message before his return to China.

Many like David and Susan are faithful, obedient Christians. They have heard God speak to their hearts about the lost world. They have prayed the words of the prophet Isaiah, "Here am I. Send me." But the door for overseas ministry seems to remain closed year after year. Too often Christians who have this experience internalize guilt or feel they must not be good enough for God to use. After all, if they were truly useful to the kingdom, God would have opened a door by now for them to go.

Another false interpretation that is made, because of the way we tend to glorify overseas missions with a certain mystique, is the erroneous conclusion that lack of an open door stems from a lack of spirituality. It is tempting to feel that those who are laboring overseas are somehow more spiritual or a cut above the average believer who remains at home.

Nothing could be further from the truth. We must make room in our understanding of God's dealings with us as laborers that he does not call every believer to a career in overseas work. In fact, there is only one difference between the missionary that is "over there" and the missionary that is "here." It is that the one "over there" is "over there." Surely

David and Susan's ministry to the Chinese at their local college is as much a step of obedience and fulfillment of their call as going to China.

Missionaries on Our Own Campuses

Wouldn't it be great if God used us to touch the lives of international students on our campus? thought a few of the college students from Redwood Chapel Community Church in Castro Valley, California. Many of them attended Cal-State Hayward, a state university with about 600 international students from all over the world.

Soon the dream became a reality, when three of the college students began a Sunday morning class called English for Internationals (EFI), to assist students with their command of the English language. Through this class some of the international students that were regulars grew more deeply involved with American Christian college students, building genuine bonds of friendship and sharing.

One night the group of students was sitting around the living room of an American home playing a conversation game called the "Ungame." Roseanna Chan, a student from Hong Kong, drew her question card from the stack. The card read, "Share one thing you are thankful for with the rest of the group." In a matter-of-fact tone, Roseanna said, "I am most thankful for becoming a Christian." The Americans around the circle looked at one another in bewilderment, because for months they had been praying for Roseanna's salvation.

"When did this happen?" one of them asked Roseanna.

"Oh, I accepted Jesus on my own a couple of months ago," she said.

"Why didn't you tell us?" came the next question.

Roseanna smiled and said, "Well, because no one asked."

Still another asked, "What made you take this step?"

Roseanna looked down and said with a smile of calm joy on her face, "It was because of all of you. I could not deny the love of Jesus in all of you, and I knew He was real and that I needed what you all have in your life."

Missions is about people. Someone once said that every person's life is like a book. A book has a beginning and an ending and tells a story as each new chapter unfolds. The exciting thing about each life is that its story is not finished. While God sees our lives from beginning to end, every life can be influenced for good or for bad.

It is in the intersection of our stories that the future is born. As God brings people across our path, we are changed by them and we are used by God to shape and change others. Missions is nothing more than those of us who carry the story of Jesus, in our story, going to those who have not yet encountered Him. It is our privilege to help their story intersect with the life-changing story of Jesus Christ. His story will change their future forever. And we have the privilege of putting their hands into his.

We don't need to be called by God to a foreign land to be used by him in his plan for reaching the nations. Ethel Hatfield, David and Susan, and the college students of Redwood Chapel Community Church are on the cutting edge of what God is doing in missions today. They simply took the story of Christ with them to those from other nations who haven't had the opportunity to meet Jesus Christ. Their trip to the mission field didn't entail quitting their jobs, or uprooting their family to settle in another part of the world. The door of missions opened for them onto a nearby campus or the dormitory of their local university.

Apply What You've Learned

1. Has God burdened you for a particular country or group of people? Go to your local university or college and see if there are students enrolled from that country. Begin to pray for them.
2. If there are students from a country for which you are burdened, offer yourself to the foreign student advisor as a friendship partner or a conversation partner. Tell the foreign student advisor you have a special interest in friendship with a student from that country and ask to be matched up or introduced.
3. Invite students from that country to your home. Allow them to bring a friend with them.

FOUR

Friendship and Blind Spots

"Even now the reaper draws his wages, even now he harvests the crop for eternal life, so that the sower and the reaper may be glad together. Thus the saying 'One sows and another reaps' is true. I sent you to reap what you have not worked for. Others have done the hard work, and you have reaped the benefits of their labor."

John 4:36–38

Our culture and neighborhoods have grown distant. People in apartments rarely know the names of their neighbors—much less have a friendship with them. We've increasingly grown more isolated.

Dr. Richard Halverson, former chaplain of the U.S. Senate and former board member for International Students, Incorporated, said, "Friendship! What a beautiful, uncommon word! Uncommon, not because it is rarely used; uncommon because it is rarely used in the context of personal evangelism."

He continued, "Most personal evangelism—as I have observed it for over fifty years—is something 'done to' someone with whom the personal evangelist has little relationship—certainly not friendship. Tragically, zealous personal evangelists often reject those who refuse to respond favorably to their evangelistic advances, thus alienating the target."

Consider the life of the Lord Jesus Christ. He made an intentional effort to be a friend to people like Matthew, a tax collector, or the woman at the well, a Samaritan. Through his friendships, Jesus Christ loved people into a relationship with God.

Friendship evangelism isn't complicated, but it means what it says— it is a friendship *and* it is evangelism. One element without the other falls short of the guiding purpose of the relationship.

John is an outgoing person and forms relationships easily. But if you ask John to talk with his friends about Jesus Christ, he falls into silence and doesn't know where to begin.

On the other end of the spectrum is Tim, who has gained a reputation for being a vocal Christian. For almost any topic, Tim finds a spiritual connection and steers the conversation accordingly, without any sensitivity toward the other person's faith relationship or cultural background. When it comes to evangelism, Tim is like a bull in a china closet. He's bound to break whoever he contacts rather than move toward a relationship with eternal significance.

One of the most helpful tools to understanding the concept of friendship evangelism is *The Spiritual Awareness and Growth Chart* developed by Dr. James F. Engel (see p. 55). This tool clarifies the big picture of moving a person from a casual friendship to a personal relationship with Jesus Christ. Students who have been raised under the communist system, particularly, have no conscious awareness of a Supreme Being. Other students may have some exposure to religion but no real knowledge of God. Many Muslim students have a positive attitude toward discussions about God even though they have no information about the Good News of Jesus Christ.

The spiritual journey for each international will be unique. Someone at −10 on Engel's scale—or no conscious awareness of a Supreme Being—could take a long time to move into a personal commitment to Christ. On the other hand, some internationals have had a great deal of contact with other Christians and may be very close to committing their lives to Christ.

If you have the opportunity to help an international move from a −10 (no conscious awareness of a Supreme Being) to a −6 (awareness of the fundamentals of the Gospel), you can be greatly encouraged. That is a great deal of progress. With the guidance of the Holy Spirit, our job is to discern the spiritual position of the student in their journey and then lovingly help him or her further along the way. Often we face confusion about our involvement with evangelism. We hang our heads in failure if we do not lead a person into a relationship with Jesus Christ. *Successful evangelism is when a Christian is available for God to use in another person's life. Through your availability, you help the other person move in a positive direction, whether or not that means coming immediately into a relationship with God.*

Spiritual Awareness and Growth

God's Initiative	Christian's Responsibility		International's Response
		+10	Vision for future ministry
	Ministry outreach	+9	Effective outreach to others
	↑	+8	Development of Christian leadership
		+7	Growth in total stewardship
Witness of the Spirit	Christian fellowship	+6	Recognition and utilization of spiritual gifts
		+5	Understanding and application of Bible doctrine
↑	↑	+4	Growth in Bible study
	Personal growth	+3	Conceptual behavioral growth
	↑	+2	Adoption of Christian identity
		+1	Assurance of salvation
Gives spiritual life	Harvesting		**Conversion: New Creation in Christ**
↑	↑	-1	Repentance
		-2	Decision to act
Convicts	Cultivating and watering the crop	-3	Recognition of personal problem in relation to God
↑		-4	Positive attitude toward the Gospel
	Planting the seed	-5	Grasp of fundamentals of the Gospel
	↑	-6	Awareness of fundamentals of the Gospel
		-7	Developing positive attitude toward God
Reveals himself		-8	Questioning present religious concept of God
	Preparing the soil	-9	Religious awareness, but no knowledge of God
		-10	No conscious awareness of supreme being

Adapted and used by permission of Dr. James F. Engel

Sometimes in working with an international, you will have the opportunity to build on a spiritual relationship that someone else has helped to develop. Jean-Claude, a young university student in Switzerland, suffered from deep depression. The despair reached the point where Jean-Claude decided to end his own life. After buying a gun, he selected a peaceful place by the river and left goodbye notes to his family.

While en route to this secluded spot, Jean-Claude was approached by a woman he had never met before. "Did you know that Jesus Christ loves you and that he wants to be a part of your life?" the woman said with a warm smile on her face.

Her words riveted Jean-Claude's feet to the ground so that he was unable to move forward. The woman told Jean-Claude about a God who desired a relationship with him. She explained, "My husband is a pastor in the city of Lausanne. Would you like to come home for dinner?" Without knowing why, he accepted the invitation. During the evening, he poured out his troubles, including his plans to commit suicide. Although the pastor and his wife helped Jean-Claude reach stability and get through his crisis and depression, he did not commit his life to Jesus Christ.

Two years later, at a university in California where he was attending a short-term English program, Jean-Claude sat on a bus. As the bus made a routine stop, a young Chinese girl boarded and sat next to Jean-Claude. He noticed a Bible on her lap and it vaguely reminded him about the pastor friend and his wife in Switzerland. Then the girl spoke to Jean-Claude: "Did you know that God loves you and has a wonderful plan for your life?"

For the next half hour on the bus, the two discussed spiritual things. "Have you ever heard of the group International Students, Incorporated?" she asked Jean-Claude. "They have a wonderful group on campus with students from all over the world. You could join one of their Bible studies. You must call their leader." Two nights later, Jean-Claude called the ISI staff member and went to his home. He recounted his spiritual journey from depression and the two people who had talked with him about Christ. That night with the ISI staff member, Jean-Claude attended an evangelistic meeting in a local church. Ken Poure, director of Hume Lake Christian Camp, clearly presented the Gospel of Jesus Christ. Jean-Claude knew that God was speaking to his heart. During the invitation, he was the first to go forward, with tears in his eyes. He had finally found the peace and forgiveness that he had sought for many years. Long before we have the opportunity to reach out to international students, God is at work in their hearts, weaving a tapestry of relationships, experiences, and people to bring students to Christ.

Friendship evangelism works differently for every student because the spiritual awareness of each can be at a different level. In some parts of the world, such as Latin America, Africa, or Korea, evangelicalism is strong. Possibly your international friend has already made a personal commitment to Jesus Christ. Ask about the specialized ministries available to this student in their home country when they return. Maybe God will use you to challenge your international friend to have a vision for a new ministry with his own people. You can be a part of the discipleship and training of your friend so that when he returns, he can make a significant spiritual impact in his own country.

Blind Spots

One evening, Bill had scheduled dinner with his Japanese friend, Nobue. Since it was getting late, Bill decided to drop by Nobue's apartment on the way home from work to pick him up.

As Nobue opened the door, a look of horror passed across his face as he saw Bill dressed in his business suit. "Please, Bill, I cannot come to your house now. Can you please wait and come back in one half hour? Then I can come." Puzzled but not wanting to pry, Bill said, "That will be fine. I'll be back in thirty minutes."

After Bill left, Nobue stripped off his jeans and T-shirt, showered, and selected his nicest suit to wear for the formal dinner that Bill and his family had obviously planned for the evening. Since Bill had thirty minutes to spare, he went home and slipped into casual clothes for the evening before returning for Nobue.

Imagine the shock for both Nobue *and* Bill when the student opened his apartment door. Bill wore jeans and a T-shirt while Nobue was dressed in his finest formal attire. Now they laugh over this story and love to tell it to others when they discuss the necessary adjustments for each other's culture and expectations.

It is fun to relate to someone from another culture, but it can take a little effort for both parties to overcome differences and unique blind spots. As English-speaking Americans, we approach life from our own experience and perspectives. Think back to the first time you got behind the wheel of a car. It's doubtful that you were aware of your own blind spots. Remember how you practically jumped out of your skin when you glanced over your shoulder on the freeway and unexpectedly saw another vehicle?

As we approach sharing our faith with someone from a different culture, we have our own distinct differences or blind spots. Unless we recognize and conquer these problem areas, they will hinder our effectiveness in a cross-cultural ministry.

Blind spot #1. We minimize our cultural differences.

There are profound cultural differences between ourselves and internationals. Our nation is based on a Christian heritage and basic understanding of the Bible and its values. Many other cultures lack this Judeo-Christian approach to life and moral issues.

When you compare North America to the rest of the world, what cultural differences immediately come to mind? To start your answer, think about some other religions in the world, such as Buddhism, Islam, or Hinduism. (For brief profiles of various religions, see Appendix A or *The Compact Guide to World Religions*, by Dean C. Halverson.[1])

According to George Barna, president of Barna Research Group, nearly nine out of ten adults (87 percent) state that their religious faith is very important in their lives. In his book *The Index of Leading Spiritual Indicators*, Barna says, "Few Americans doubt that God will judge every individual. Almost nine out of ten people (87 percent) contend that eventually all people will be judged by God."[2]

Our culture generally accepts the idea that God exists, people are sinful, and that Jesus Christ is a historical figure. Each of these concepts may be completely foreign to your international student. Be careful not to load your conversation with commonly used religious terms and assume your friend will understand you. At the same time, don't hesitate to talk about your faith. The Good News about Jesus Christ is the power of God for salvation. Often the international student will initiate a conversation about religion, faith, or spiritual things. It is common for students to be open to discuss this subject with an American.

Keep in mind two distinctions about this particular blind spot:

- The ideological walls that separate people from different cultures and religions are real.

- These walls rarely crumble with a single conversation. Rather, they must be eliminated, brick by brick.

Blind spot #2. We don't understand our audience.

We tend to act as though everyone approaches life from our cultural perspective. An excellent resource for learning about spiritual and cultural differences is *Operation World*, by Patrick Johnstone.[3] This book, as well as the previously cited *Compact Guide*, will help you understand the political, social, and spiritual climate of other countries.

When we fail to get to know our international friend's customs and culture, we demonstrate this second blind spot and can make simple mistakes. For example, during the Christmas break, the Jenkins family invited a Japanese student to stay with them in their home. Each morning Mrs. Jenkins changed the towels in his bathroom and to her chagrin found that he had taken a bath but not emptied the water in the tub. Also, the tile floor was covered with water. The first day she attributed it to forgetfulness and emptied the tub and mopped the floor.

But her frustration increased when this pattern continued through the week. She thought the Japanese student either lacked manners or was lazy. Actually, Mrs. Jenkins felt angry that the student expected her to clean up after him. The least he could do was empty his own bath water.

The problem was Mrs. Jenkins did not understand Japanese culture: one washes his body outside the tub, rinses off with water on the tile floor, then gets into the tub to soak. Homes in Japan have drains built into the floor to carry away the water. Because the hot water in the tub is clean, it is left for other family members to use for soaking. To empty the tub before several have used it is considered wasteful.

Similarly, it is easy for us to misinterpret actions, words, and customs. Too often we look at a situation through our own culture's eyes and attribute ill motives, judging others accordingly. If we don't anticipate the possibility of differences, we can damage relationships. We need to "think the best" and then allow room for correction of what is usually a misunderstanding. Through openness and discussion we can learn and make the necessary adjustments.

If we are sincere in our desire to befriend someone from another country, then our first step is to become familiar with his country, culture, and family. Your international student is the best person to help you learn these cultural differences. Take a learning posture and let him teach you about his world.

Some questions to ask might be:

- What's your country like?
- What would you like us to know about your family?
- What do you like about the United States? What don't you like?
- What actions have we Americans taken that you find offensive?
- Are there some cultural differences in particular that you would like to tell us about?
- How can we meet your needs? Tell us how we can best help you and be friends with you.

As you seek to learn more about your international friend, it will draw you closer together and make your relationship more natural and more enjoyable. Through your genuine interest, you may also gain the opportunity to meet the student's spiritual needs by tactfully applying the Gospel of Jesus Christ to his or her own cultural grid.

Remember that even though students may call themselves Muslim or Buddhist or Hindu, they are not necessarily religious. For this reason, it is important not to push the student to defend the religion of his family or nation. Such a tactic is likely to alienate him or her from the Gospel.

In many other places in the world, religion and culture are one in the same. For example, in many European countries, the people belong to the state church even though it has no spiritual significance in their daily life. Many internationals see America as a Christian nation in the same way we see Saudi Arabia as an Islamic nation or Thailand as a Buddhist nation. The student's perception of Christianity is often based on what he sees on television, in American films, magazines, and even life in the university dormitory. You can help them understand that not everyone they meet in America is a Christian.

Sadly, after their experience in American universities, many Muslim women return to their homeland with a new commitment to Islam. Their exposure to the typical American has convinced them that they do not want to become Christian and that Islam is a better way of life.

Blind Spot #3. We view evangelism as an event.
The Christian church has perpetuated the concept that evangelism is an event rather than a relationship. Years ago, the church encouraged

enthusiasm through annual or semi-annual evangelistic meetings. Today we still gather unsaved friends and take them to large crusade meetings where major evangelists are speaking. While these events are crucial and give an opportunity to begin a personal relationship with Christ, they are not enough. Evangelism should become a lifestyle and not be focused on an event.

In Acts 26:12-18, Paul tells of Jesus meeting him on the road to Damascus. Jesus said, "I am sending you to them to open their eyes and turn them from darkness to light, and from the power of Satan to God, so that they may receive forgiveness of sins and a place among those who are sanctified by faith in me."

These words of Jesus explain three stages of evangelism. *First* we need to open the eyes of the people. The Word says that the truth sets us free in Christ. Often the Bible uses metaphors related to farming when it comes to evangelism. The process of opening another person's eyes to the truth of Jesus Christ involves forming a relationship. Friendship evangelism in the early stages involves learning about that other person. As we become acquainted, we build the opportunity to talk about spiritual matters. To put it into the farming metaphor, this process is like plowing. We open a relational opportunity for dialogue about spirituality and God.

The *second stage* of evangelism is "turn them from darkness to light, and from the power of Satan to God." After forming a relationship, we need to tactfully discuss spiritual matters with the international student, or "plant" truth from God's Word into his heart. As the word of God works in a life, it leads the individual to turn from evil and to an awareness of the need for a Savior—Jesus Christ.

The *third stage* is "so they may receive forgiveness of sins and a place among those who are sanctified by faith in me." If your friend has arrived at this point in his spiritual journey, you may lead him in a prayer of commitment to God and to a personal relationship with Jesus Christ. Follow up his decision with a study of the basics of the Christian life. One way to accomplish this is through the video *New Beginnings*. It includes fifteen minutes on each of seven topics: salvation, assurance, lordship, the Holy Spirit, prayer, the Bible, and witnessing. (See appendix for more information.)

As we have said before, evangelism is not a single event, but a process. As an essential step in the process of friendship evangelism, you will need to determine the spiritual awareness of your international friend. Determine this before you begin to communicate spiritual truth. It's impossible to reap a harvest where no seed has been planted. You may befriend a Chinese student who has never even talked with a Christian. Or befriend a Muslim who believes Christians worship three gods: God, Jesus, and Mary. If the overconfident friendship partner attempts to lead a Chinese or Muslim student to Christ without first assessing the student's spiritual knowledge, he will only encounter frustration and confusion and perhaps alienate the student.

Each of us bears a responsibility as an ambassador for Jesus Christ. As we seek to work with the future leaders of the world, we do not want to say or do anything that would hinder their spiritual journey or create negative feelings about Christians or about God. Prematurely pushing a student to make a decision for Christ can have a damaging effect if he is not ready. Our task is to remain sensitive to God's Holy Spirit and his leading.

Dr. Feng, a slight Chinese man in his mid-fifties, had been in the United States for nine months when he visited the International Students, Incorporated Embassy West Coffee House in a major northwestern city. He had earned a master's degree in archaeology in the People's Republic of China, and a Ph.D. while studying in the Pacific Rim. He was offered a professorship at a university in mainland China but had given up that position to come to the United States with his wife and nine-year-old child. His wife was involved in a post-doctorate fellowship at another northwestern university.

Dr. Feng's English was somewhat limited, and he spoke to an American Christian in the coffee house through a Japanese interpreter. (This type of cross-cultural interaction isn't unusual.) In his zeal to share his faith, the Christian was less than sensitive in this case, and asked Dr. Feng abruptly, "Do you know that you are a sinner?"

The question came as a total shock to Dr. Feng, because to him, being Chinese, the word "sinner" meant "criminal." He answered, "No, how could I be? If I were a 'criminal,' I would be in prison and not in the United States." From his religious frame of reference, Dr. Feng had no theology of sin.

The interpreter was stuck and tried to explain to Dr. Feng what it meant to be a sinner, but to no avail. Out of frustration, the Christian handed Dr. Feng a Chinese Bible in simplified script. He told him, "Please read this. It will help you understand what I am talking about."

During the next few weeks, Dr. Feng read the entire Chinese Bible several times! Later, he said that he understood who God is and that he himself was a sinner. From the Bible, Dr. Feng understood that he could be forgiven for his sins, and he received Jesus Christ. In addition, he helped his wife and child to personally know the Lord.

As Dr. Feng looks back at his spiritual journey, he feels that God brought him to America and to the Embassy West Coffee House in particular so he could learn about the Creator God. From his study of archaeology, Dr. Feng came up with some unanswered questions, such as why there was a great flood throughout the world and why China had some of it's origins in Iraq, or the Mesopotamian area.

Dr. Feng had been taught that men came from apes, but he knew this could not be true because, he said, "apes begat apes and humans begat humans." To explain the evolution of humans from apes, Dr. Feng was told that humans evolved because of labor. Apes are tool users and came out of trees. Then they used tools to dig out honey from trees and ants from ant hills. Through using their minds and tools, apes evolved into humans. According to Dr. Feng, this theory is believed by about 80 percent of all Chinese, but he could never make sense of it. As he read the Bible, Dr. Feng's studies in archaeology made sense. Science helped him in his pilgrimage to Christ as Lord and Savior.

While the American in this story didn't have a perfect balance of spiritual sensitivity, God used him in spite of his mistakes and through the Scriptures led Dr. Feng and his family to a personal relationship with Jesus Christ. Again, we need to be sensitive to the spiritual condition of the international student before we begin our friendship evangelism.

Blind Spot #4. It depends on me!

We need to understand the importance of our relationship with an international student, but balance is crucial. We tend to overplay our role in the student's making a personal commitment to Jesus Christ. Remember: we communicate truth, but God saves. Our understanding of this blind spot means keeping two things in perspective:

1. Patience and proper timing are critical if the seed of Gospel truth is to take root and grow. As the apostle Paul taught the church at Corinth, "The Lord has assigned to each his task. I planted the seed, Apollos watered it, but God made it grow" (1 Corinthians 3:5-6).

It's important not to become either overconfident or oversensitive in your friendship partner relationship. For example, an overconfident friendship partner meets Fang Yi from China. Without seeking basic information about Fang Yi's spiritual background, he plows ahead and pushes her to make a commitment to a personal relationship with Jesus Christ. Fang Yi fails to understand the cost of becoming a Christian. If she converts to Christianity, she will probably do so because her culture constrains her to please her American friends and not lose face. Her commitment will not be out of conviction of a genuine need for salvation but out of obligation to please.

The opposite could also occur if a friendship partner is oversensitive. Aware of the cost for an individual from a Communist country to make such a commitment, the oversensitive friendship partner may make no effort to speak of a commitment to Christ because he or she doesn't want to threaten the friendship. The result is that a person such as Fang Yi would have no concrete witness and no opportunity to seek God for salvation through Christ.

As we seek his will, the Lord will open natural opportunities for us to talk about our personal relationship with Jesus Christ or to study the Bible with an international so he or she can make their own decision. Our first need is to be willing servants. God will take our willingness and our reliance on the Holy Spirit and guide into all truth.

2. When it comes to international student evangelism, we must remember how successful evangelism is determined. It is not only when a student makes a personal commitment to Christ. Success is responding to the leading of the Holy Spirit. Jesus said, "I sent you to reap what you have not worked for. Others have done the hard work, and you have reaped the benefits of their labor" (John 4:38).

German students Ulrike and Irmgaard lost their baggage and money while traveling in Canada. A Christian family came to their rescue, brought them home, and bought new clothes for them. A month later, they stayed in a youth hostel in Oregon. Unknown to the girls, the hostel was run by Christians. The host couple told Ulrike and Irmgaard about Jesus Christ. Two weeks later, while hitchhiking, the girls were picked up by two widows who drove them down the west coast to San Francisco. During the trip, the two older women shared the love of Christ with the girls. When Ulrike and Irmgaard reached San Francisco, they wrote the couple in the hostel and told them they had both accepted Jesus Christ. God uses many people in the chain of events to bring students into a personal relationship with Christ. The theme at International Students, Incorporated, is 1 Peter 3:15, in the J. B. Phillips version: "Quietly trust yourself to Christ your Lord, and if anybody asks why you believe as you do, be ready to tell them, but do it in a gentle and respectful way."

We need to faithfully turn our lives and spiritual conversations over to the Holy Spirit and trust God to bring "success" from our faithfulness. Success is simply being a part of the process and the chain of events that brings Christ to an international student as his personal Lord and Savior.

Blind Spot #5. We have a narrow view of evangelism.

Cross-cultural evangelism with international students involves a variety of approaches. Too often the words "evangelism" or "witnessing" evoke the image of a person with an open Bible in his hand, verbally challenging someone with the Good News about Jesus Christ. Evangelism is much more complicated than this stereotypical image. We will cover evangelism in depth later in this book, but for now we need to recognize various avenues of witness to international students.

Life Witness

Brenda Korsten grew up in a church with a strong missions emphasis, but she never dreamed she could have a missionary impact without ever leaving home. As a college student, Brenda saw international students every day from all over the world. When her church began an outreach to international students, Brenda became a small group leader for a weekly English as a Second Language class that met at her church.

Margaret, a speech pathology major from Taiwan, attended Brenda's group to work on her vocabulary, but after a few weeks she had to drop out because of a conflict. It was a painful decision for her, because Margaret really wanted to be a part of the class. Sensing an opportunity to serve, Brenda offered to meet individually with Margaret on a weekly basis. She would give her the new vocabulary words and review the lesson from the previous week.

After a month of sessions, Margaret said, "Why do you do this for me? You faithfully come every week, without pay, and you don't even know me. You are a very decent person, Brenda."

Margaret's question opened the door for Brenda to share the Gospel and explain that her actions came from her love of Jesus Christ. Not long afterward Margaret's father died in Taiwan. His death triggered a wrestling over many internal issues. "I'll never be good enough to please God," Margaret said to herself.

Feeling sad and lonely, Margaret said, "Who can I turn to? There is only one person—Brenda. She will listen and help me." Through that phone call, Margaret found Jesus Christ. Through Brenda's selfless service and sacrificial lifestyle, the Gospel opened a door in Margaret's heart. Repeatedly, international students who have found Christ say that seeing Jesus in the life of their American friends brought them to where they could not deny their own need for Jesus in their life.

As Joe Aldrich says in his book *Lifestyle Evangelism*, "People don't care how much you know until they know how much you care."[4]

Kalila found comfort in her new American friends. Much of what she saw in American culture disturbed her. From the Middle East, Kalila was often shocked by the loose morals and behavior in the media and in everyday dormitory life at the university. While she did not understand what made her friendship family different, she found similarities in their family life to the values and devotion of her own Islamic faith. She felt their home was a refuge from the negative side of the American culture, a side that her own religion would not have tolerated.

As the months passed Kalila attended many family functions. Her friendship family made her feel like part of their family. She was even invited to their childrens' birthday parties and large family gatherings with grandparents, aunts, uncles, and cousins.

One thing that intrigued Kalila was the family's devotion to spiritual things and their commitment to their holy book—the Bible. They were what was called in Islamic culture, "People of the Book," even if their book was not the Koran. In her heart, Kalila knew that they lived what they believed and she admired their love for one another and commitment to family life. Her curiosity started many conversations about their Christian beliefs. Kalila felt a freedom to ask questions because these friends never pushed their faith on her. She was aware that they wanted her to know about their faith and that it was central in their life, but they never pressured her. Kalila also knew in her heart that they loved her for who she was—no strings attached.

On Easter Sunday, Kalila attended the church musical with them. It was a phenomenal presentation about Jesus' death and Resurrection. As they left the parking lot to go home, Kalila began weeping—first silently, then audibly sobbing. Surprised and concerned, Robert pulled off to the side of the road.

"Kalila, what is wrong?" he asked.

Trying to regain her composure, she spoke in a whisper, "I know that the story of Jesus we saw today is true and I know I need him in my life like you have him in you and your family . . . but I cannot accept him. My family will never understand if I become Christian. I know it is true because I see Jesus real in you and the other people, but to accept him, I must say to myself everything I have ever believed from my life in Iran is not correct. Islam is my life."

The life witness from this family brought Kalila closer to the truth.

Students who come from nations with little or no Christian heritage are attracted and most receptive to this style of evangelism. 1 John 3:18 says, "Dear children, let us not love with words or tongue but with actions and in truth."

Your lifestyle can testify to the goodness and grace of the Lord Jesus Christ in your life.

Verbal Witness

Our verbal witness is when we talk about our personal relationship with God through Jesus Christ. This verbal witness can take place in many different forms. One is telling the international student about your own spiritual journey. Another would be to go through a tract or booklet such as *Knowing God Personally* (see Appendix A), or watching the *Jesus* video together and using the ISI study guide. You may want to study a pre-commitment Bible study together (see Appendix B). Each of these methods for verbal witnessing will be explored in depth in the chapter on evangelism. The international students who are most receptive to this particular approach are "prepared people" or students who over time have been exposed to Christ through the Bible and His people.

Corporate Witness

Life-changing power is also revealed when an international student sees a community of faithful believers in Jesus Christ. A church that has genuine worship and caring relationships within the congregation is the best place for this type of witness. For corporate witness to work in the life of the international student, you will need to go with the student to church and introduce him to your Christian friends. The reality of such loving relationships will be observed not in a single meeting but over a period of time.

Luke records the impact of corporate witness in Acts 2:42–47, and concludes by saying, "And the Lord added to their number daily those who were being saved."

A survey was conducted among students who had converted from Islam to Christianity. They were asked why they finally became Christians. Their answers emphasized the importance of corporate witness: they cited unexplainable answers to prayer and the unmerited acts of love from Christians. The average length of time between their first introduction to Christianity and their conversion was seven years.

Friendship evangelism is a process and not a single event. As we understand the different approaches to evangelism and the variety of avenues for witness, we will have more tools at our disposal for reaching international students with the Good News of Jesus Christ. As we recognize our blind spots and overcome them, we will increase our effectiveness in turning these future leaders toward a spiritual relationship with Christ.

In summary, here are some basic do's and don'ts for friendship evangelism:

Do:

- Be committed for the long term—trust takes time.
- Be a genuine friend and don't base your friendship on the student's spiritual interest.
- Take an interest in the whole person and the variety of the person's needs.
- Know your student.
- Learn from your student.
- Build a true friendship (going out of your way to sacrifice and give).
- Share your faith gently and respectfully.
- Find points in common for an ongoing relationship.
- Pray *with* the student and *for* the student.
- Accompany the student to church.

- Trust God to work.

  Don't:

- make any assumptions
- argue
- pressure a student to make a decision
- take the student only to Christian activities
- assume that church is the only place where the student will hear and understand the Gospel
- give up!

A Ministry for Everyone

Everyone can have a ministry to international students. In the next chapter, we'll go into more specifics. Whether you are young or old, single or married, widowed or recently remarried, if you have a willing heart, you can be friends with an international student. The next chapter will detail part of the range of experiences you can have with an international student. It will also explain the lost art of hospitality and the distinction between it and entertainment.

The Perfect Family Ministry

Often families are divided by their desire to reach the world for Christ. Mom attends a women's conference, while Dad is involved in a Promise Keepers meeting, and the children are in their youth program. A friendship partnership with an international student is a ministry in which the entire family can participate.

For nearly eight years, Jim and Sue Comfort, along with their four daughters, have been reaching out to international students in Castro Valley, California, through Redwood Chapel Community Church. As Jim says, "Nothing can provide your family a better missions experience than reaching out to international students."

He continues, "It's one of the most affordable and effective ways to teach your kids the importance of reaching out to people from other cultures. Our children have a genuine sensitivity and acceptance of others because they realize that God has made all of us the same way and with the same basic needs."

Their daughter, Brenda, says, "Our family is very family-oriented and this has been a great ministry to do together. We've had the opportunity to share our faith in the process." The oldest daughter, Wendy, went on, "Some of the students have even stayed with us, like Keiko, an author from Japan. Our family developed enough relationship with her that she invited me to Japan and paid my expenses to come and stay with her family. The fact that we are an openly Christian family opens doors for us to share what makes our family different."

Another friendship partner had international students from Indonesia visiting their family. Derrah and Pam could not understand why two women in their thirties were having so much fun playing with their seven-year-old son and his friend. To their surprise, they learned both of these international students had sons the same age that they had not seen for eighteen months because of their studies! As these women stayed overnight, Derrah and Pam had an opportunity to talk about Christ during their regular family devotions. It was a natural means to talk about spiritual matters. The children in your home and the way they are treated will speak volumes to students about their spiritual needs.

Here's a series of action steps to take with your family as you consider becoming a friendship partner.

1. Gather as a family and discuss your involvement as a friendship family with international students. Survey each family member to see how they like the idea, then secure their support and excitement.

2. Pray with your family about your involvement, and ask for God's direction.

3. Trust God for your family's ministry in friendship to international students. Understand that the benefits to your family will probably outweigh the benefits to the student. Some of these benefits include:

- knowledge of another culture
- training for your children in geography and customs of another country
- having a new friend from a faraway place
- encouraging a missions emphasis in your family
- learning about the food and the language of another culture
- seeing how God is at work in other lands
- God's blessing as you *give* without motive to *get*
- developing closeness in your family as you minister together

- becoming foreign missionaries right in your own home
- requires reasonable amounts of time
- having your family become a model ministry family within your local church.

4. Contact ISI for your Volunteer Training Kit (see Appendix A).

5. Review the training kit and share it with your pastor.

6. Contact your local international student ministries representative, or the foreign student advisor, whose names are noted in the Volunteer Kit, along with information for contacting these people.

7. Become acquainted with your international student through an evening meal, and let him or her train you by asking questions about their family, country, culture, and personal goals.

8. Begin your international friendship (whether you are a family, a single person, a family with children, a retired family, or a senior citizen without a spouse). International students are lonely and hungry for relationships. In addition, they want to know the American culture and the American way of life. Although they may not assimilate it, they are curious, and we have an opportunity to assist them.

9. Feel free to call ISI (1-800-ISI-TEAM) at any time for counsel and advice about this relationship or further training (see Appendix A for ISI contact information).

To sum up, remain faithful to your international students in times of stress and personal trials as well as joy. Be willing to be with them when family members overseas are going through great difficulties and the students feel alone and need your help and prayers, and perhaps condolences. You will be just a phone call or an e-mail contact away.

Communicate with your international student and follow up if they move to another school or when they return home. International students are often from very close-knit families. Consequently, friendships with them are very meaningful, deep, and rewarding. Be their friend. You will find this reality as you take time from the very rigorous pace of American life, shift your priorities, and give yourself to them as a true friend. They are generally sensitive, caring, loving, appreciative, and responsive. Their friendship will enhance your life immeasurably.

Apply What You Have Learned

1. Do you struggle with unfulfilled ministry or service desires and expectations in your life? Take a few minutes in prayer and ask God to

replace those desires and expectations with a new vision. Perhaps you made a childhood commitment to go overseas and were sidetracked somewhere in your career. How can friendship evangelism with international students give you a fresh opportunity to reach the world for Christ?

2. Review the five blind spots when it comes to working with international students. Which blind spots are evident in your own life?

3. How can you overcome these blind spots? Part of the answer may come by reviewing the do's and don'ts section of this chapter.

4. Pray that God will help you to overcome your blind spots and give you an international student for a friendship partner.

FIVE

Entertainment or Hospitality

"Keep on loving each other as brothers. Do not forget to entertain strangers, for by so doing some people have entertained angels without knowing it."

Hebrews 13:1-2

Through their local church, Alfred and Carol had met an international student in their area. Mohammed, an Indonesian Muslim, was coming that evening to dinner for the first time.

Suddenly there was a knock at their front door. "Oh, Alfred, it's that international student we invited."

Alfred frowns. "It's about time. Doesn't he know his way around here? The rolls are probably stone cold and the roast is overcooked." Alfred reaches the front door and flings it open, saying, "Hey there, where have you been?" Then he looks to the kitchen and shouts, "Honey, it's that international student! Come on in. Let's see now, your name is, uh . . . (he looks down at a card) . . . how do you say it?"

"Mohammed," the student says with confidence and a smile.

"Huh?" Alfred looks puzzled. "Well, let's call you 'Moe.' Come on inside, Moe, and have a seat. I hear you are from Indonesia. Isn't that somewhere in Africa? Or is that Indochina—I'm still mad about that war we had over there."

Mohammed sits down in the living room and with embarrassment looks at the floor. "Well, it's really—"

Alfred interrupts, "I see. Well, listen, Moe, we have a great evening lined up for you. Carol is fixing our all-time special meal—pork roast!

Then after dinner, we can turn on the TV and watch the Giants kill the Patriots. Monday night football is an American tradition that you should know about."

Now Mohammed looks even more confused, saying, "But, sir, I can't eat—"

Making no attempt to listen to what his guest is trying to say, Alfred interrupts again, "Sure you can! I know you must be hungry . . . I'm starved. We'll eat in a minute, but first I want you to know how special it is to have you here in our home. You know, God has blessed this country of ours, and I know you will come to see that Jesus Christ is really the Way, the Truth, and the Life. Aren't you glad that God is finally going to show you the True Path to Him, and wash away your sins through His blood?"

Now it's Mohammed's turn to frown and he tries to begin again to squeeze in a word of conversation. "We Muslims believe—"

Like a jumping bean in a jar, Alfred skips to the next question on his mind: "That brings me to another question. I know it's awfully hot in your country. Do people wear shoes? And do you live in grass huts or what?"

Carol calls into the living room, "Dinner is on the table."

Alfred puts his arm around Mohammed and continues telling him how great the pork roast will be.

If you follow the example of Alfred and Carol, you will do irreparable damage to an otherwise enjoyable relationship. While we may chuckle at this story, virtually all of the mistakes that Alfred made have also been made by well-intentioned Americans who are cross-culturally insensitive. Take a few minutes to consider how Alfred and Carol fell into the series of blind spots outlined in the last chapter.

There Is No Need to Be Afraid

In our culture of fast food and instant meals, some people are petrified at the thought of entertaining someone from another country. What does it involve? In the minds of some people, such entertainment requires an extremely high personal standard. For their house to be perfect, they will need to either hire a maid service or spend a week doing spring cleaning. Some people feel they need to use the formal dining room with the best china and glassware. Because people with these expectations have set such a high standard for entertaining, they will likely never take advantage of the opportunity to have an international student in their home.

Students are not looking for high-quality entertainment. They are looking for simple hospitality and friendship. One Sunday an ISI family had Daphne from Japan in their home for lunch after church. Following a time of conversation, the family was ready for their customary Sunday afternoon nap. They explained to Daphne, "We are going to rest now." If she wished, she could also rest on the couch. For the next two weeks, this family heard reports of how Daphne proudly announced to her student friends how much she felt a part of the family. She had never taken a nap before in an American home, but this family felt free to include her in their regular routine. A nap could hardly be considered impressive or special, but Daphne felt honored to be treated as part of the family.

Throughout the New Testament, we are encouraged to offer hospitality to others. "Offer hospitality to one another without grumbling" (1 Peter 4:9). "Share with God's people who are in need. Practice hospitality" (Romans 12:13). Beyond the confines of hospitality to fellow Christians, we are to reach out to nonbelievers and in particular to international students.

"But I don't know how to cook," you moan.

With a bit of preparation, it doesn't have to be complicated. The student will be delighted to participate in your family meal—provided you prepare in advance for your first meeting. If you are too busy to cook, you can invite your guest to a restaurant for dinner and possibly to your home afterward for conversation.

Before the First Meeting

Perhaps through your church, or through International Students, Incorporated, or the Foreign Student Advisor on campus, you've been given the name and phone number of a nearby international student.

Your first step should be prayer. Ask God to prepare you and the student for the first meeting. Pray that you will approach the situation with spiritual sensitivity and a willingness to express a balance between friendship and evangelism.

When you receive the name and country of the student, locate the country on a world map and discover something about it—their religion, politics, economics (see Appendix A for resources).

When you call the student and invite him or her to your home, be specific about the time you will arrive if you are to pick the student up. If the student is female and you are a man, make sure that your wife or children are along with you; if your student is male, and you are a woman, make sure your husband or children accompany you, to avoid the possibility of a misunderstanding. Single friendship partners should only be matched to students of the same gender.

Let the student know what you will be doing and what type of dress would be appropriate. If you have difficulty reaching the student, the best time to call may be between 10:00 P.M. and midnight, the time when most students return from the library. When you do reach your student, find out what is the best time to call in the future.

Your first meeting doesn't have to be some special event. Plan to include the student in things you normally do as a family such as dinner, a ball game, a day at the park, or a trip to the museum or zoo. He or she will not want to be entertained or singled out. Rather, the student generally wants to experience normal American life. Remember to include the student in your holiday celebrations such as Thanksgiving or Christmas, and be ready to answer a lot of questions about American culture!

During the First Meeting

When you meet your new friend, enjoy getting to know him. Learn to say his name correctly. If his name is Mohammed, call him Mohammed. Don't use a nickname, unless he asks you to. Don't ask questions that could be insulting, such as, "Do they drive cars in your country?" He may normally have a chauffeur!

The next chapter includes a number of conversation starters to help you get to know your student friend.

In many countries, conversation is a form of entertainment. Your student is probably used to relaxed conversation. He or she will be especially interested in talking about his or her family and homeland.

You may be presented with a gift. Accept it graciously and be aware that the custom for opening gifts varies in different countries. Feel free to ask what is appropriate. For example, in parts of Latin America, the recipient of a gift doesn't open it in front of the person but waits until they leave. In America, we like to see the expression of the person opening the gift, so we generally open it when we receive it. Ask the student about their cultural expectation: "If I were in your country, would I open this now, or after you leave?" and then act according to the response. You should be prepared for the fact that he or she may bring you an alcoholic beverage.

Before meals, you can say, "It is our custom to thank God for our food." Don't simply bow your head and begin talking. Also, don't change your normal routine for a meal. If you have children, they will let everyone know that what you are doing is different than normal!

Usually we encourage our guests to serve themselves first. But don't ask the international student to go first. He or she probably doesn't know what the foods are or how they are intended to be served or eaten. It helps to explain what the different foods are and to show how they are served and eaten.

In some cultures, it is considered impolite to accept seconds until you are asked several times. Help your student understand that the American custom is to help oneself or accept the invitation for seconds the first time it is offered.

Some students will not be comfortable around pets, especially if they are in your house. In fact, Asians and Africans can be terrified of pets, and for Muslims it is taboo and offensive to have pets in the house. It is best to keep your pets away from the student until you know how he feels about them.

In some cases, the student may be a smoker. If it is your family's practice not to allow smoking inside the house, offer to step outside with him or go for a walk.

When talking with the student, speak slowly and distinctly. Do not raise your voice. The student isn't deaf just because he or she has an accent! Be careful not to use idioms or humor or Christian clichés (see chapter 6).

Make sure you explain the significance of different holidays. Can you imagine someone arriving at your international friend's door dressed as a ghost on October 31? Unprepared, the student could be terrified at the American cultural tradition of trick or treating.

Do not ask the student to baby-sit your children. Despite their attraction and relationship with your children, each culture maintains different values. Your request could lead to a rift in your friendship. Also do not allow your children to ride in a car that a student is driving. His or her concept of safety may not coincide with yours.

During your conversation with the student, don't mention that you have missionary friends in their country. You don't know the student's opinion of missionaries or experience with them. If that experience has been negative, it could hinder your new friendship. Or possibly your missionary friend is in the student's country to teach English or work at a business. If you reveal their missionary purpose, it could risk their expulsion from that nation. While you don't want to talk with the student about your missionary friends, you may want to talk with your missionary friends about the student. Then the missionary could initiate friendship with your student when he returns home.

Make a point to listen to your international friend's perception of life in America. He or she may be experiencing culture shock and your friendship can help him or her adjust to the culture. The following is a graphic illustration that shows the felt needs that all international students have in common. Understanding these basic needs will enable you to be a helpful friend to your student.

As the graph below illustrates, students need a friend as soon as they arrive in the U.S., and especially during the first six months. Otherwise, without a friend, a student may be a lonely "foreign" student during all

---

What International Students Are Saying About Their Needs and Concerns

Homesickness

Food

Language difficulties

Medical services

Financial problems

Future vocational plans

Developing friendships

Everyday problem-solving

Social relationships with the opposite sex

Obtaining housing/adjusting to new housing

Maintaining cultural and religious customs

Unfriendliness of community/violence/racism

Adjustment to new customs and new educational system.

A. Church, (1982) "Sojourner Adjustment," Psychological Bulletin. 91.E540–572

T. Stafford, *The Friendship Gap: Reaching Out Across Cultures* (InterVarsity Press, Downers Grove, Ill., 1984).

their years in our country. He or she enclaves only with his or her own people and never experiences the "international" environment. This happens often; let's be that friend and offer the gift of our culture as a part of the student's overseas experience.

Don't promise the international student that you will do something with him unless you actually plan to do it. We are prone to say things like, "Let's get together next week" or "We'll go to the lake sometime." The student will expect that you are going to follow through with the plan and feel confused or hurt if you do not.

Continuing Your Friendship

The Smiths were thrilled! The ISI team leader from their church had matched them with a student from Indonesia to come to their home for Thanksgiving. As they dropped Suleman off at the dorm after a wonderful day and a traditional turkey dinner, they told Suleman how much they enjoyed hosting him and how they looked forward to getting together with him again. They gave him their phone number and told him to call anytime if they could help with anything.

Weeks passed and during a friendship partner sharing time with the other friendship partners from their church, the Smiths discussed their sadness with the rest of the group. It had been almost two months since they heard from Suleman. They couldn't understand it because they had had such a wonderful time on Thanksgiving Day, and he seemed to enjoy their family.

Unfortunately, the Smiths had the false expectation that it was Suleman's turn to call them. In our American culture we have come to expect reciprocation. When we invite someone to an activity, we subconsciously expect contact back from them as a sign for the relationship to continue. With international students, this is almost never the case.

For the student, living in another culture is enough of a challenge, much less taking the initiative to call or reciprocate. As the American hosts, we need to take the initiative and set up time together. This will be true long into the relationship. Many cultures would deem it forward or improper to impose oneself on an American friend. That is why a lack of initiative on the part of a student should not be interpreted as a lack of interest. More than likely they are wanting to continue the relationship with you and are hoping that you will seek them out.

Trust takes time. Ask God to give you the grace to persevere with your friendship through the challenges of communication and scheduling. It's important that you count the cost of a continuing friendship and not begin one unless you can faithfully meet with the student on a monthly basis and call him regularly throughout at least one school year.

As your friendship grows, share more about your own personal life. As you risk new topics of conversation and are open to the student, it will permit him to share his deeper feelings with you. Be careful not to be dogmatic about your opinions on such controversial topics as divorce, abuse, abortion, or politics. Many students will have experienced some of these things in their own life, and if they perceive you will judge their experience negatively, they will never share deeply with you.

Allow the student to initiate expressions of friendship to you. One ISI couple, Tom and Jean, met Dimitri from Russia. Before becoming a student in the U.S., Dimitri had been a tank commander in Siberia. As Tom and Jean's family opened their home and shared freely with the young man, he expressed a desire to return their kindness by cooking a Russian meal.

So the date was set and other American friends were invited to experience this culinary feast. Realizing that Dimitri lived on a limited budget, Tom and Jean asked for a grocery list for the meal for twelve and purchased the supplies ahead of time. On the appropriate evening they greeted Dimitri warmly, then stepped out of his way. The young chef went to work.

The meal was a delight; the food was excellent. The chef glowed. What an experience! And it is one many friendship partners can enjoy.

Pray daily for your new international friend. Get together with him regularly, and call him to see how he is doing. Find out your student's birthday and plan to do something special. Many countries do not celebrate birthdays. You may have the opportunity to give your friend his first birthday party!

One key to a successful friendship with an international student is to *relax*. If you make a mistake, it will not create an international incident! Laugh at yourself. It will become the great leveler of cross-cultural differences. Your friendship could be one of the most exciting adventures of your life. And you never know the long-term effects of your friendship on the international.

Activities to Strengthen Friendship

The building block of a developing friendship is a shared event—particularly when that friendship is based on the love of Jesus Christ. The following activities give you an opportunity to know each other in natural ways. You can anticipate many opportunities for sharing Christ's love both in word and deed through shared experiences. Use these pages as a resource guide but feel free to expand the list and explore other possibilities. You'll notice most of these ideas are simple and easy to accomplish. They will keep your friendship moving in the right direction.

Communication

- Pray daily for your friend.
- Visit with him in person once or twice a month.
- Make weekly contact by phone or letter or e-mail.
- Ask about his or her birthday—send a card; plan a party.

Family

- Meals—entertain at different times, not only at dinner.
- Family celebrations—birthdays, holidays, special events
- Family outings—picnics, visiting friends and family, shopping
- Overnight stays—especially during school breaks
- Tour of your home—ask about what may be unfamiliar.
- Visit the student's apartment and meet his or her friends.
- Ask your friend to cook a national dish for you.
- Teach how to use your favorite recipe.
- Make your home a place to relax and be at ease.
- Integrate your friend into the family routine.

General Helps

- Invite your friend to church but don't force or insist (inform beforehand of the purpose of the program or event).
- Help with conversational English and writing skills (offer to proofread papers).
- Give a Bible as a gift, preferably in the student's language, and offer opportunities for study.
- Give your student the *Jesus* video and study guide in his or her own

language (see Appendix A for resource guide).

- Write to his or her family and friends overseas, describing mutual activities.
- Take pictures for the student to keep or send home.
- Interpret American customs.
- Share problems and needs; develop a good listening ear.
- Help him or her find warm winter clothing or other special needs.
- Find out what are his or her favorite activities and sports.

Resources from International Students, Inc.

An extensive resource list is found in the final pages of this book. Here are some relevant resources for strengthening friendship.

- Give the student *How to Survive in the USA* (see Appendix A).
- Invite the student to ISI functions, holiday conferences, and fellowship groups to meet other internationals.
- If your student is moving to another location within the U.S., use ISI's national network to link your friend with other Christians.
- When your student returns to his home country, link him with other Christians through ISI's overseas network.

Places to Go and Things to Do

Like the previous list of ideas for strengthening your friendship, the following list will generate more possibilities. When you are stuck for an idea, turn to this resource. Each of these activities or places will strengthen your relationship with an international student.

Athletics

- Attend amateur or professional games.
- Observe children's sports.
- Attend university or college sporting events together.
- Join a city sports league and play together.
- Watch events on television.
- Ask your student to teach you a national sport.
- Work out together at a gym or the athletic center of the college or university.

Trips Out of Town

- Visit relatives.
- Take mini-vacations together.
- Take camping trips and visit national parks.
- Take sight-seeing trips to historical locations.

Places to Visit

- Scenic locations in the area
- Historical sites
- Recreational areas
- Specialty shopping (Chinatown, Japantown, antique stores), or traditional American shopping

Fun Activities

- Holiday celebrations (use any occasion)
- Picnics and festivals
- Weddings/special family events
- Fairs
- Art exhibits
- Parades

Visiting

- Relatives and friends
- Friends with vocations of interest to the student
- Friends with special hobbies and/or talents

Short Visits

- Visit locations on campus where your friend studies or works.
- Drop by with baked goods or small gifts.
- Meet him or her on campus for a cup of coffee or a soda.
- Visit your work location and introduce your student to co-workers.
- Attend a lecture or other cultural events together on campus.

Outdoor

- Hiking, biking, walking together
- Camping

- Outdoor concerts
- Lakes, parks, waterfalls
- Fly a kite.
- Play catch or tennis.

Build a Relationship Around the Table

Inviting your international friend for a meal is a wonderful way to strengthen your relationship. As you become better acquainted, you'll learn the types of foods your friend likes and dislikes, and also his or her favorites.

Although we may not think of them as such, meals are a key part of our culture. Families and friends fellowship and interact around meals at home, eating out, having coffee or snacks together, or picnics. The following recipes and insights will help build confidence to develop your relationship with the international student around the table.

Dietary Restrictions

The dietary restrictions of an international student may be religious, cultural, or individual. The following recommendations are generalizations and don't pertain to every person in a given group. Religious dietary restrictions depend on how strict an adherence one has to his or her religion. A good rule of thumb is, if in doubt, ask!

- Hindus and some Buddhists generally do not drink beer, while many Germans drink it as a regular beverage served with a meal.
- Some Hindus and Buddhists are strict vegetarians. They eat no meat, fish, poultry, eggs, or dishes containing any of these ingredients.
- Muslims and most Jews do not eat pork of any kind.
- Some devout Muslims may not eat any form of beef, lamb, or poultry, unless it has been butchered in a specific manner. Fish is usually acceptable.
- Many international students will not eat chopped and/or processed meats that contain unknown ingredients.
- Many Asians and Africans do not care for cheese or canned tuna.
- Some international students avoid diary products or are unfamiliar with them.

What to Serve

In general, chicken, rice, fish, fruit, and vegetables are good choices to include in a meal. Casseroles are usually not familiar or enjoyed by internationals. It is a good idea to have a bottle of hot sauce on the table. Many cultures prefer their food hotter and spicier than Americans.

The following are basic guidelines for meals.

- Rice is a staple food in many cultures.
- Vegetables and fruit—fresh, canned, or frozen—are generally appreciated.
- Chicken is a favorite. In many countries, it is served with rice.
- Fish, seafood, lamb, and cheese may be acceptable alternatives for those who don't eat beef or pork.
- Many prefer simple fruit desserts or ice cream to rich or heavy pastries.

We include below six tried and true recipes we've found to be winners with international students from around the world. Each of these meals are easy to prepare. Of course, individual preferences will vary.

Lazy Lasagna
(Serves 4-6)

1 lb. ground beef or Italian sausage
8 oz. package shredded mozzarella cheese
8 oz. package mini lasagna noodles
28 oz. jar Italian Spaghetti Sauce

Brown meat. Cook noodles as directed on the package. Set aside some cheese for topping and mix remaining ingredients together into a large dish. Top with extra cheese. Bake at 350° for 30 minutes, or until cheese is completely melted. (Note: You can leave out the ground beef or sausage for a delicious vegetarian main course.)

Quick Turkey Curry
(Serves 4)

¼ cup chopped onion
1 T. butter
1 can condensed cream of mushroom soup
¼ cup milk
1 cup dairy sour cream
½ tsp. curry powder
1 cup cubed, cooked turkey
Snipped parsley

Optional condiments: sliced water chestnuts, raisins, toasted slivered almonds, sliced green onion, or mixed pickles.

Cook chopped onion in the tablespoon of butter. Add cream of mushroom soup and milk. Heat and stir until smooth. Stir in sour cream and curry powder. Add cubed turkey; heat. Garnish with snipped parsley. Serve over hot cooked rice. May offer optional curry condiments listed above.

Ten-Minute Chicken Dinner
(Serves 6)

2 whole chicken breasts
2 T. salad oil
1 green pepper, cut into strips
1 small onion, sliced
1 cup diagonally sliced celery
1 can (5 oz.) water chestnuts, strained and sliced
1 cup chicken stock, divided
1 tsp. Accent (optional)
1 T. sugar
½ tsp. ginger
2 tsp. cornstarch
2 T. soy sauce
1 can (16 oz.) bean sprouts
1 pkg. (6 oz.) chicken-flavored rice, cooked according to package directions

Cut meat from bone; cut into small shreds. Cook chicken in hot oil in skillet until white (about 3 minutes). Add green pepper, onion, celery, water chestnuts, ½ cup of chicken stock, Accent, salt, and ginger. Cover; cook until vegetables are crisp-tender (about 5 minutes). Mix cornstarch with soy sauce and remaining ½ cup stock. Add to skillet with bean sprouts, stirring until thickened (about 2 minutes). Serve with hot cooked chicken-flavored rice.

Five-Minute Skillet Dinner
(Serves 4-6)

2 cans (7 oz. each) tuna in vegetable oil
1 cup diced celery
⅓ cup chopped onion

1 medium green pepper, diced
1 pkg. (6 oz.) herb rice, cooked according to the package directions
⅓ cup diced pimiento
1 can (3 or 4 oz.) sliced mushrooms
1 tsp. each: salt, pepper, rosemary, marjoram
⅓ cup slivered almonds

Drain tuna oil into skillet; heat. Add celery, onion, and green pepper; cook until vegetables are crisp-tender (about 3 minutes). Add tuna, hot cooked herb rice, pimento, mushrooms, and seasonings. Heat to serving temperature. To serve, sprinkle with slivered almonds.

Meatless Vegetable Curry
(Serves 4-6)

1 can (1 lb.) small white potatoes
1 T. flour
1 can (8 oz.) small green peas
1 can (16 oz.) cut green beans
1 can (20 oz.) chick peas
½ tsp. each: chili powder, turmeric, Tabasco, Accent (optional)
¼ tsp. coriander powder
⅛ tsp. ground cumin

Drain liquid from potatoes, reserving ⅓ cup. Combine reserved liquid with flour to make a smooth paste; set aside. Drain liquid from remaining vegetables into a skillet. Boil rapidly until liquid is reduced to 1 cup. Stir in spices and Tabasco. Blend in flour paste and stir until slightly thickened. Add vegetables and Accent; heat to serving temperature. May be served alone or with rice. (Note: 2-3 tsp. curry powder may be used instead of spices listed.)

Fruit Salad
(Serves 8-10)

2 red delicious apples
2 green pears
2-3 bananas
2 T. lemon juice
2 cans mandarin oranges
2-3 cups seasonal fruit (fresh peaches, grapes, melon, etc.)

Cut fruit into bite-sized pieces. Mix together with lemon juice. Add or omit fruit according to personal tastes, but pay attention to the color combination. Prepare close to serving time and refrigerate.

In these last few pages, we've clarified some activities and the difference between entertainment and hospitality. One of the critical elements of hospitality is conversation. When you get together with a student, what do you talk about? The next chapter will give some ideas for conversation starters.

Apply What You've Learned

1. How do you distinguish between entertainment and hospitality?
2. Make a list of ideas you've gleaned from these pages that you can use. What two or three ideas will you apply this month?
3. Expect a fun-filled time with international students. Let them cook a meal for you and share their culture.
4. Make a list of family activities and events that will occur over the next six months, and decide in which you could include your international friend.

SIX

Jump-Start Your Conversation

"Wisdom is supreme; therefore get wisdom. Though it cost all you have, get understanding. Esteem her, and she will exalt you; embrace her, and she will honor you."

Proverbs 4:7–8

"But when he asks, he must believe and not doubt, because he who doubts is like a wave of the sea, blown and tossed by the wind."

James 1:6

Throughout his years of schooling, Max has always been a bit shy. Now he's begun a friendship with Pedro from Colombia, and he wonders what in the world they will talk about. Max likes the idea of an international friendship and wants to share his faith, but he's also uncomfortable with silence in their relationship.

Most international students enjoy the opportunity to speak with Americans. The sincerity, patience, and understanding of your communication is a very important part of building a new friendship. These guidelines, while basic, have proven to be helpful to many Americans as they form friendships with international students.

Listen attentively. In conversation with your international friend, remember that listening is an art and takes effort. When you listen attentively, you are paying him or her a high compliment by showing your genuine interest and concern.

Speak carefully to be understood. Remember that your new friend may be limited in his knowledge of English and may not fully understand what you are saying. Articulate your words and speak slowly and clearly.

Avoid idioms or slang. Your conversational English is probably quite a bit different from the classroom English your friend learned in his or her homeland. Idioms and slang are particularly perplexing for the international. Imagine what mental images are stirred in your friend's mind by phrases such as "play it by ear" or "kill some time." If you do use idioms or slang, explain what these phrases mean. As you speak, make direct eye contact and pick up on any nonverbal clues that you are not being understood. Encourage your friend to ask you about expressions you use that he or she doesn't understand. We have included some cartoons that illustrate some English idioms. Show them to your new friend as a conversation starter.

Use jokes and humor sparingly. Because international students lack the cultural context and immersion in the English language that we possess as Americans, they may have difficulty understanding jokes or humor. If you do use jokes or humor after your friendship is established, make sure you explain them when necessary. Avoid teasing. Those from other cultures may take this as an insult or be offended due to lack of understanding.

STICK YOUR FOOT IN YOUR MOUTH

To say something that is incorrect or embarrassing.

Explain words and phrases patiently. Invite your friend to ask you about words or phrases he or she does not understand. As you speak, carefully and patiently explain anything you think was not understood. A puzzled look, an inappropriate response, or a hesitancy to answer can be a cue that the student did not understand you. When this happens, repeat yourself, using different—perhaps simpler—words. Do not raise your voice to make a point. The student may interpret this as impatience or condescension. Explain the use of slang or idioms that will help them converse with others on a day-to-day basis.

Respect differences of opinion. Obviously, you and your international friend will have differences of opinion from time to time. It's important that you share what you think—honestly, but with sensitivity—and that you respect the student's ideas and opinions. Try, however, to avoid controversial subjects that may create tension or arguments.

Most international students enter this country with preconceived ideas about American life. These ideas can be traced to movies, magazines, the news media, propaganda, and observation of Americans abroad (some of whom may have been poor examples). Some international students arrive in the United States already suspicious and envious of the prosperity enjoyed by most in this nation. Other students have a difficult time separating our government's political and military policies from Americans in general.

An international student's homeland may be either pro- or anti-American. The country may be old, with an established culture and history dating back thousands of years; or it may be new, struggling to establish its identity. These factors will certainly influence your conversation on certain issues (see Appendix A for country profiles).

As your friendship with the international student deepens, so will your mutual trust. He or she will become more willing to discuss personal or semi-controversial subjects. As you become acquainted with your friend, you will want to learn a great deal about him or her. In the following pages, a number of conversation starters are included. Add your own topics to these pages. A key to stimulating conversation is to avoid asking simple questions that require yes or no answers. Rather, utilize who, what, when, where, and how questions for good conversation.

Another caution is to avoid sounding like a talk-show host or an interrogator. Include more than one international in conversation, when possible, to promote interaction between cultures and countries represented.

To the church at Colosse, Paul wrote about good conversation, saying, "Let your conversation be always full of grace, seasoned with salt, so that you may know how to answer everyone."

Geography

- Where is your city? What is it like (large, small)? What kind of climate do you have there? Can you show me where your city is on a map?
- Describe the appearance of a typical home in your country. Which is usually the largest room in the residence? Are there extended families living together or nearby?
- Describe your country's physical features (mountains, lakes, deserts, forests, rivers). What is the physical environment around your home?
- Are there national parks, historic places, and recreational areas that you have visited in your country? What are some of the most interesting?
- What would you like to see while you are in America?

Photographs/Family

- Do you have family photos that I could see? Show family photos of your own.
- Compare and contrast photographs taken in this country with photographs of your friend's country.
- Watch a video or a film from the library on American life and culture, national parks, scenery, or other points of interest.
- Ask family-related questions: How large is your family? What is your position of birth in your family? Which family members live at home? What kind of work does your father and/or mother do? What is your extended family like?

Language

- What languages do you speak? How long have you been studying English?
- Ask how to say various greetings and other common phrases in his or her language, such as, "Hello, how are you?" "Please," "Thank you,"

and "Goodbye." Write them down phonetically, and practice saying them with your friend.

- Learn how to write words of greeting or other expressions in his or her language.
- Offer to help with any expressions or concepts in English with which he or she is having difficulty. Explain American slang and jokes.

TO OPEN A CAN OF WORMS

To create several more problems while trying to solve just one.

Money

- Ask to see currency used in his or her country.
- Discuss how his or her money corresponds with U.S. currency according to the exchange rate.
- Inquire about the cost of food, gasoline, housing, and other things in his country. How does the cost of living in his country compare with that of the U.S.?
- Find out if your friend has had any difficulties getting money from home or getting money exchanged. Maybe you can be of help.
- Ask about trading corresponding coins as mementos of your friendship.

Socializing, Dating, and Marriage

- In your culture, how do young men and women get to know each other? Are marriages arranged?
- At what age do young people begin dating? Do you and your friends go out in groups or as couples?
- At what age do most couples marry? Does the father (or both parents) need to give permission to marry?
- What are some of the wedding customs?
- If you are planning to serve a meal at 7:30 P.M., at what time do you ask your guests to arrive? If a friend invites you to a party that begins at 8:00 P.M., at what time do you plan to arrive?

Family Life

- What roles or functions do the father or mother perform in the family of your culture?
- What influence do older people, such as grandparents, have on their adult children and grandchildren?
- What responsibilities do children have in the family?
- What are the holidays in your culture, and how do families celebrate them? Which holiday is your favorite?
- Where did you grow up—in the city or in the country? Who does most of the cooking and housework in a typical family? Tell me about your parents' daily lives.
- At what age do children start school? How many hours per day?
- How are children disciplined for disobedience?
- What is the average number of children in a family?

Men's and Women's Roles

- What kinds of work do men traditionally do in your country?
- What kinds of work do women traditionally do?
- Do women hold political office in your country? How long has this been acceptable? What do you think about it?
- Are women included in your country's armed forces? If so, in what capacities?
- Do married women work outside the home? If yes, do husbands assume additional responsibilities at home?

- Who is the head of the family unit?
- How do you feel about the role women play in American culture?

Recreation

- What games do children play at home? At school?
- What games do junior high and high school youth play?
- What are favorite adult forms of recreation in your country?
- What are popular recreational activities for families?
- Does your country have a national sport? More than one?

Education

- What are some differences between your educational system and ours?
- Are teaching methods different here than in your country? If yes, how do they differ?
- Do you have difficulty understanding your professors here? Are they sensitive to your problems? If yes, in what ways?
- How are students chosen for high school and college or university in your country?
- How much does it cost to attend high school or a college or university in your country?
- What degrees are most popular or valuable in your country?
- What degree are you pursuing?
- How would you evaluate the education that you are receiving here?
- In what ways do you hope to apply the education you are receiving here when you return home? How long do you expect to study here?
- Is it possible for students in your country to transfer educational credits over here?

Transportation

- Do you have an international driver's license? How does a person obtain one?
- What experiences have you had in getting your driver's license? (Note: Many international students will not have driver's licenses; some have never learned how to drive.)
- What differences are there between driving here and driving in your

country? (You might discuss rules and regulations, driving habits, and so forth.)

- Do most people drive in your country? What kind of cars are most common? How do automobiles in your country differ from those here?
- Is a pedestrian given more or less consideration in your country? Please explain.
- What other modes of transportation are common in your country besides automobiles?
- In your country, how do you get to school or work? Do people travel much from town to town?
- How do bus and train travel in this country compare with that in your homeland? How much does it cost to use a taxi or local bus in your country?
- Is it customary for a family to go somewhere for a vacation?

HIT THE ROAD

To leave.

Food

- What was your first reaction to American food? Has anything surprised you about American food? How do you like it? Do you have a favorite dish?
- What are the staple foods in your country? Which of these are grown locally and which are imported? What foods does your country export?
- Are your foods highly seasoned? If yes, which seasonings do you use?
- What is your favorite food in your country? How is it prepared? Would you like to use my kitchen to cook sometime?
- Do you cook your own meals here? If so, are you able to buy the ingredients you need? Which ones are hard to find?
- What beverages do people in your country drink?
- Where do you usually eat, in your apartment or out?
- What is a typical breakfast, lunch, and dinner in your country? Does the family eat together most of the time?

Spiritual

- Religion can be a sensitive topic for discussion. Make sure you've established a foundation of mutual respect and trust. Many cultures are less sensitive about discussing religion than people in the United States. Feel free to develop your own questions, but be careful about when and how you ask them. And remember not to press for answers.
- I'd like to learn more about your religious beliefs. Would you be willing to share something about them with me? Is there something about your religion that is very important to you? (If yes, listen attentively. If no, politely move to another topic.)
- What do you believe is the meaning of life?
- What is your concept of God? May I tell you mine?
- Before you came here, what did you know about Christianity?
- Has anything you've learned about the Christian faith since you've been here surprised you? If yes, what?
- What is your perception of religion in this country?
- How do people in your culture worship? What are your worship centers like? What are some of the religious customs? (Be willing to share some American religious customs as well.)

- Would you like to attend church with me sometime? (Don't pressure your friend but offer the opportunity.)
- Would you like to study the Bible together? (See Appendix B for suggested Bible studies.)

Cultural Sensitivity

Cultural sensitivity is a key ingredient to good conversation with an international student. While a cultural anthropology course is outside of the realm of this book, there are a number of key issues related to increasing our sensitivity. If we approach internationals with these elements in mind, we will be less likely to hinder the relationship and, in fact, will build a deeper relationship.

One Thanksgiving, four international students attended a seminar entitled *The Search for Freedom*. Each student came from a different part of the world—a Marxist from China, a Muslim from Mali, a Buddhist from Japan, and a black from South Africa. At the beginning of the seminar, each student was asked to define freedom.

The Chinese Marxist said, "Freedom is the absence of capitalistic exploitation."

The Muslim from Mali replied, "Freedom is to escape unbelief through submission to Allah."

The Japanese Buddhist confidently said, "Freedom is to be free from desire."

"Freedom is to break the power of racism," concluded the South African.

Notice how each student defined freedom from his or her own worldview. Our belief system, background, and environment have deeply shaped who we are as people—in fact, values can be so ingrained we don't even think about them or challenge them or realize there may be an equally reasonable way to think.

Without knowing it, each of us has become ethnocentric, or has the tendency to view his or her culture and way of life as normal and a standard for judging other people. Because of our own ethnocentrism, we tend to view people from other countries as different, strange, or even wrong.

Before we can become more sensitive to other cultures, we must understand our attitude toward our own culture. Each of us holds many beliefs, habits, and thoughts about life that are cultural rather than right or wrong. We need to recognize that other cultures have equally valid means and ways of doing things. When we do, we come to appreciate people from other cultures.

Following is a sample list of values that many Americans hold as important contrasted with what are frequently non-Western values:[1]

American Values	Non-Western Values
nuclear family	extended family
individualism	group most important
written language	legends and stories
social mobility	no career changes or "getting ahead"
technology	relationships
progress and change	family and stability
time efficiency	resistance to change
romantic love	arranged marriages
democracy	socialism, communism, dictatorship
free market	business is cooperative—strategic alliances
youth	age and wisdom
directness	passiveness in problem solving
worth in terms of achievements	people more important than production
competition	equality
dichotomization	religion and culture may be one
entertainment is bought	conversation is entertainment
reasoning in terms of probability	reasoning in terms of known
distrust of authority	submission to authority
privacy	socialization
personal problem solving	corporate problem solving
goal orientation and control over future	fate has predetermined the future

As we increase our awareness of these cultural differences, it helps us become more sensitive to the student. The values in this list are neither right nor wrong; they are simply different. For the student, these distinctions may create an experience of deep culture shock.

Student Culture Shock

Culture shock is the emotional upheaval that comes from negative feelings a person experiences while adjusting to life in a different culture. The phenomenon comes in two stages for the international student. At first they may think the people and culture in general are quite similar to their own—initially they don't notice all the differences. Then it gradually dawns on them that these people and this culture are indeed [very] different from their own. Herein lies the shock.

A Christian international student, Elaine, arrived on her Tennessee campus from Malaysia. During her first few days, Elaine stayed in a motel near the university and searched for an apartment. She recalls, "I felt lonely, miserable, and homesick to be on my own. I was so upset, depressed, and frustrated in that motel room, as I didn't know people or how to get around, and everything was so expensive that I felt like giving up. I asked myself, *How could God possibly send me thousands of miles away from home and yet not provide me with accommodations?*"

Then John Eaves and his wife invited Elaine to stay in their home. With these new friends, Elaine walked through her culture shock. Now she says, "I am staying with them currently, and Mr. Eaves is helping me look for a place to stay. I am following them to church on Saturday nights and it is a real miracle for me."

Signs of Culture Shock

Culture shock can be evaluated and observed in your student. Here are some physical and emotional signs:

- strain—so many psychological adaptations have had to be made without any break or time apart
- sickness—headaches, sleepiness, or insomnia
- sense of loss, or feelings of deprivation with regard to status, friends, possessions, food, housing—to which they have been accustomed
- overeating or not eating
- rejection—being rejected by members of the new culture and/or rejecting members of the new culture.
- withdrawal—they may not respond to your efforts to help or relieve and, in general, their desire to be with other people is greatly diminished.

- feelings of discrimination
- confusion—in roles, expectations, values, feelings, and self-identity
- frustration—may result in their verbally tearing apart the U.S. culture
- anger
- surprise, anxiety, disgust, and indignation
- feelings of powerlessness—due to fear of not being able to succeed in the new culture

When you see your student suffering culture shock, there are two possible solutions to the crisis:

1. Time. Like anything new, it takes time to adjust.

2. Break the routine. Actively doing something to learn about their new culture is helpful. In any case, it is a critical time, and the student needs your friendship and concern.

Stages of Culture Shock

As you develop your friendship with the international student, it is helpful for you to recognize the different aspects of culture shock.

The first stage is called the *honeymoon stage*. During this time, the student experiences many similarities to his or her own culture. He or she is excited with the newness and adventure of living in the United States. This stage can last from a few weeks to several months. The primary time for bonding and developing a lasting friendship is during the honeymoon stage. The earlier we get involved in the life of an international student, the easier he or she adjusts, and the greater our opportunity for impact on their life.

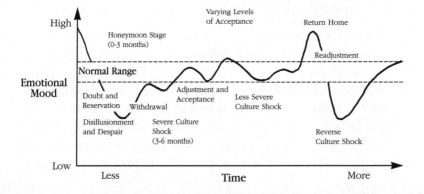

Doubt and reservation mark the second stage. The student begins to ask questions like, "Why did I come? Will I ever fit in? I have a doctorate in engineering at home, so why can't I understand engineering here? The language is so difficult."

As culture shock intensifies, it moves into the third stage of *disillusionment and despair*. Severe culture shock may hit around final exam time. It's helpful for you to know and understand these low times in a student's life so you can understand the impact it has on your friendship evangelism. You may feel the student is resisting your invitations because of busyness or stress or fear of failure, when in reality it is the time when your student needs you the most.

Withdrawal is the next step in the downward spiral. At this point, you may need to take a more aggressive role in fostering your friendship. It helps to understand this stage and the ensuing resistance rather than being put off by it.

You must take a proactive role in helping the student through this withdrawal stage. Go to the student's dorm room or apartment and take him or her out for ice cream or to the park. Insist on making a time to get together, then stick with it. Send notes of encouragement. More important than anything at this point: *Don't give up*. The friendship can easily end at this juncture if you do not understand the emotional needs of the student.

The final stage of culture shock involves *adjustment and acceptance*. Each student will respond with varying levels of acceptance, but almost every student will adapt to their life in the United States. If he or she is here for a short time, there will be more resistance to adapting than if he or she plans to be here for a longer period of time.

The Importance of Nonverbal Communication

Whether we realize it or not, 70 percent of our communication is nonverbal. It is important in our dealings with international students that we be aware of our other expressions.

First, we communicate nonverbally in the area of *body language*. Our posture, gestures, and movements indicate a great deal of information. Simply the way we sit or move communicates certain degrees of acceptance and enjoyment of the situation in which we find ourselves. For example, how do you feel when you are talking with someone and he crosses his arms? What does this gesture indicate to you?

Eye movement and position is another area of nonverbal communication. In America, it's important to maintain good eye contact with the other person during a conversation. If someone does not, we sense either disinterest in us or lack of self-confidence on the part of the individual. However, in many cultures, individuals never look at each other. You may particularly notice this aspect with students of the opposite sex; they may feel it is inappropriate to look you directly in the eye.

Touch is a nonverbal communication skill. But we need to be careful and sensitive in this area—who, where, when, how, and how much, are all culturally distinctive when it comes to touch. Some cultures kiss on the cheek—including those of the same sex—each time they greet. Others, particularly older Asians, almost never touch someone of the opposite sex in public.

Personal space, particularly the amount needed, varies drastically from culture to culture. We have a comfort zone in which we feel at ease relating to others. If someone moves too close, we automatically take a step backward. However, if he or she is not close enough, we tend to feel a sense of rejection. For Americans, this personal space is about an arm's length, but in some cultural groups the person needs to be close enough to smell your breath! Personal space is an important factor in developing cultural sensitivity.

Formality and informality is another area of distinction among cultures. Americans tend toward a more informal lifestyle. Generally, there is flexibility in social situations in regard to dress, and through that flexibility we show the value we place on individuality. By contrast, in some cultures—Japan, for example—formality in dress, in language, and in greeting another shows respect for the host or declares one's social status.

Time perception is the final area of nonverbal communication. What does it mean to be "on time"? Western culture runs by the clock, whereas other cultures do not and generally place more value on relationships and less on time and events.

Value the Other Person

As we relate to the international student, our emphasis is on valuing the person. When we are sensitive to the multiplicity of change that he or she is facing, we can appropriately share Christ's love. Understanding the phases of culture shock the student is going through will enable us to minister to them in this critical phase of life when they are particularly vulnerable. A review of the culture shock sequence will prepare you to help the student wherever they are in the process of cultural adjustment.

Cultural Role Plays

One of the best means to increase your sensitivity to other cultures is to role play with another American. Doing so may prevent you from making some major mistakes in an international friendship. Each of the following three situations can be acted out in a small group or family setting. Select one person to play the role of the international and have them read their particular part just before the role play.

Cultural Role Play #1: Read only the "situation" to the small group or family.

Situation:

An American and an international student have just been introduced to each other at a party for new students. It is hoped that several friendship partner matches will be arranged before the evening is concluded. The American wants to talk about everyday things, but the international interprets everything politically and talks about his country from that perspective alone.

Do not read the following paragraph to the others! It is information that only the "international" should know.

Cultural behavior of the student:

The student is from Hong Kong. Because he is accustomed to a great deal of noise and crowded conditions, he is very friendly, but talks loudly and rapidly (uncomfortably loud to an American's taste). In addition, the student frequently interrupts. He is close to phobic about the effects of communism and this is one of the reasons he is so focused on the political perspective of every twist in the conversation.

Choices:

You may choose the age of the student, whether he is in graduate or undergraduate school, his major, and whether he is married and has a family (and whether that family is with him in the United States).

Cultural Role Play #2: Again, read only the "situation" to the small group or family.

Situation:

For the first time, an international student has invited a fellow graduate student (American) out to lunch. They have known each other for two months and have had a few short conversations. The American begins eagerly to ask the international student questions about her homeland, but she never clearly answers the questions. The American wonders if this is because the student has a poor grasp of English, if she doesn't like being asked questions, or if there is some other reason for her behavior. The American cannot tell whether or not the international is uncomfortable.

Do not read the following paragraph to the others! It is information that only the "international" should know.

Cultural behavior of the student:

The student is from Uganda (Africa). Under the repressive regimes of dictators for the last fifteen years, people in her culture have learned not to initiate conversation or to make eye contact (it appears threatening if you are too direct) in interactions with people whom one doesn't know very well. When asked a question, the student pauses, saying nothing for a few seconds, before replying to each of the American's questions. The American typically does not wait long enough for the student to begin talking—so it appears that the student is ignoring the American's questions. (See if the American can learn the pattern of waiting for an answer longer than 30 seconds.) From this student's cultural background, it is considered wise to think about answers to questions, instead of saying the first thing that comes to mind.

Choices:

You may choose the age of the student, whether she is in graduate or undergraduate school, her major, and whether she is married and has a family (and whether that family is with her in the United States).

Cultural Role Play #3: Remember to read only the "situation" to the small group or family.

Situation:

An American friendship partner has invited the international student with whom he or she has been matched to their home for dinner. It is their first meeting in the home but they were introduced a month ago.

At that time, they only had a brief conversation. At the dinner, the student constantly smiles, nods, and agrees with everything the American says. But the American senses that the international probably disagrees with at least some of the things that are being said.

Do not read the following paragraph to the others! It is information only the "international" should know.

Cultural behavior of the student:

The student is twenty-four years old and from the People's Republic of China (mainland China). This student was raised in a very formal atmosphere where respect for older people was almost the law. It would never enter this student's mind to disagree in public with the American because that might cause the American to "lose face"—an unforgivable sin toward another person in the Chinese culture. In fact, it is difficult for the student to look the American in the eye for any length of time—that would be too direct! In addition, though the student can write English with no trouble, his or her speaking ability is limited.

Choices:

You may choose whether the student is in graduate or undergraduate school, his or her major, and whether or not the student is married and has a family (and whether that family is presently in the United States).

After each of these role plays, allow a time of debriefing. What did you feel as an American? How did the person playing the role of the student feel? What areas of conflict came into the situation? What things did each do that bothered the other? How could you as an American adapt to build the relationship?

Beyond Good Conversation—the Art of Good Listening

Throughout this chapter, we have emphasized good conversation and increasing your sensitivity to the cultural differences of international students. Successful cross-cultural communication often involves a strong investment in the development of good listening skills. While the main objective is to encourage internationals to open up and speak, merely shooting questions back and forth can become dull. For mutual satisfaction to develop out of the relationship, you must learn to practice good communication skills. Some of the characteristics of a good listener include

- selecting topics that are of mutual interest and require more than short answers. (Make sure your surroundings are quiet enough to hear each other.)
- being alert to nonverbal cues that indicate the other person is feeling uncomfortable, and resisting the urge to speak louder if your friend finds it difficult to understand what you are saying.
- using clarification questions to promote dialogue. (Proper feedback maintains conversation.) Don't ask, "Do you understand?" Instead, ask, "Do you mean to say. . . ?" Use open questions rather than ones that require yes and no answers.
- using questions that indicate your interest in his or her feelings, such as, "How did you feel after that happened?" or "How would you respond to this if you were in your country?"
- helping to bring the conversation into focus by summarizing statements, such as, "These seem to be the key concerns you have expressed . . ." or "Your primary point seems to be. . .". Often, such statements stimulate additional dialogue or discussion.
- resisting the urge to blurt something out in order to fill the void of silence. Though silent periods may seem awkward to you, they may indicate that the student is showing you respect, is thinking about his answer, or is allowing a transition between topics.
- selecting questions that will get some mileage out of the conversation, that will indicate a greater depth of interest in knowing your student. Avoid questions that are too specific about family, or overly trite, such as, "Where is your country?" or "When are you going back?"
- being careful not to judge the quality of the relationship by how well you communicate on the same wavelength. It may take some time to adjust to each other's communication habits.
- remembering cross-cultural communication is a skill to be developed.

Apply What You Have Learned

1. Consider your own sense of other cultures. How would you rate yourself on a scale of 1 to 10 (1 being totally ethnocentric and 10 being highly sensitive to other cultures). What issues highlighted through-

out this chapter do you need to examine in your own life?

2. How can you develop skills to become a better listener? List three practical steps you will take in this area.

3. Armed with these various conversation starters, how do you feel about engaging in conversation with an international student?

4. Team up with a small group and practice the role plays in this chapter.

5. Find another American partner and take turns pretending one of you is from another country and that you are meeting for the first time. Use questions from this chapter to become skillful at conversation and listening.

SEVEN

Evangelism With International Students

"He who goes out weeping, carrying seed to sow, will return with songs of joy, carrying sheaves with him."

Psalm 126:6

"You will seek me and find me when you seek me with all your heart."

Jeremiah 29:13

About two years ago, one of our staff was speaking at the Friday night meeting for the International Christian Fellowship in Austin, Texas. Following the meeting, two young women from mainland China came to talk with him. They were both in the master's program, one in electrical engineering and the other in computer science. They asked a pressing question: "How can we know God personally?"

Despite years of experience in evangelism, he said he suddenly felt unable to respond in detail. His only thought was John 3:16. So he opened his Bible and located the passage, then turned his book around so both girls could read it with him. Then he briefly explained the meaning of the verse and how they could know God personally. Several months later, he heard from another ISI staff worker in the area that both students had made personal commitments to Jesus Christ during the following months. One student committed her life to Christ in the summer and the other in the fall. He was thrilled to have a small part in their personal and newfound relationship with Jesus Christ. A lesson learned from that situation was that God uses the scriptural truths from the Bible to bring others to a personal relationship with Jesus Christ. And that simplicity is very effective.

Bathed in Prayer

While we desire that every international student experiences personal salvation through Christ, evangelism has to be accomplished with great sensitivity and in the power and strength of the Holy Spirit. In our own strength, we can do nothing to draw another person to Christ. In the power of Christ Jesus, we can do all things because we know that nothing is impossible for God (Matthew 19:26).

As we seek to share our faith in Christ with internationals, the first step is prayer. Here are some general guidelines:

- Pray for sensitivity to know where your student is emotionally, culturally, and spiritually.
- Pray that God will move in the heart of your student to give him or her a desire to know Christ. (The simple fact that God has brought the two of you together is an indication that God is working.)
- Pray for discernment to know when there is an openness to the Gospel.
- Pray for a genuine love for your student and commitment to him or her.
- Ask your student how you can specifically pray for him or her.

Prepare to Give an Answer for the Hope Within You

To effectively share the fundamentals of Christianity, you should be able to answer basic questions about what Christians believe.

- What do Christians believe about God, the Bible, the meaning of life, mankind, sin, etc.?
- How does a person come to have a relationship with God?

- How does man communicate with God? How does God communicate with man?
- Who is Christ? Why do you believe he rose from the dead?
- If Christianity is the only way, what about my family and friends back home?
- What is the way to salvation?
- How do we know God wants a personal relationship with us?

A good study Bible will help you answer these questions and prepare ahead of time for solid answers. *The Compact Guide to World Religions* (see Appendix A) is also a good tool for understanding where your student may be coming from with regard to religion. It will be a good investment of your time to know how to give an answer for the hope that is within you.

Positive Approaches

- Ask your friend if he or she is acquainted with the Bible and to what degree. Be willing to listen—without interruption—to your friend's impressions, even if you disagree with certain comments. At this point, building your friendship is more important than correcting biblical knowledge.
- Ask the student if he or she would like to have a Bible to read (perhaps in his or her native language) or if he or she would like to study the Bible.
- Ask your friend what he or she knows about Christianity. Again in your discussion, welcome honest impressions and be prepared for a negative or positive reaction.
- Discuss basic questions:

  What do you think is the meaning of life?

  Do you know what the Bible says about God, or what God says about himself in the Bible?

  In your opinion, can we know God? Why or why not?

  Has God revealed himself to us? If so, how? If not, why not?

  What do you believe is the nature of man?

  What is sin? How can man overcome sin?

  Is there life after death? Why or why not?
- During an appropriate time, talk with your friend about what Christ

means to you personally. Point out the uniqueness of a Christian's relationship with God through Christ. (Explain the fact that God sent his Son to earth to make it possible for man to have a relationship with him, rather than demanding that man do whatever he can to reach God.)

- Answer your friend's questions honestly and diplomatically. If he or she poses a question for which you do not have a ready answer, admit that you don't know the answer, but also tell him or her that you will research the question before your next meeting. Carefully discern between sincere questions and "smoke-screen" or "roadblock" questions. Avoid being drawn into tangents.

- Many international students want to learn the essence of Christianity, but for some their interest is limited to cultural curiosity. Others will have a genuine concern for spiritual matters and a thirst for spiritual truth.

- Encourage your friend to investigate Christianity and the Bible—at least on an intellectual level. It is reasonable to expect that a well-educated person would have a basic knowledge of this major religion and of Jesus, one of history's greatest spiritual leaders. You may also point out that the Bible is the bestselling book of all time.

- As you communicate, keep Christ central in your discussions. His life and teachings are known around the world. Build on this knowledge. Talk about who Jesus is, what he claimed about himself, and what God said about Jesus through the Bible. Jesus often told stories and used illustrations to teach truth. Don't hesitate to use some of his parables and other stories. In many cultures, this approach is appreciated and easily understood.

- Concentrate on Jesus' death and resurrection. The evidence for his death and resurrection is powerful. The book *Evidence That Demands a Verdict* by Josh McDowell lists supporting sources.

- Invite—but don't pressure—your friend to attend church with you. If he or she chooses to attend, make your friend feel welcome and carefully explain the activities that take place.

Use God's Word

Carol was an international student journalist who was studying in Ann Arbor, Michigan. Some friends brought Carol to a Friday Bible study group and her life was changed forever. As she says, "I confess my spiritual life was empty. I was a Christian only by name and religion was something I would remember for Sunday! As I studied the Bible in depth for the first time in my life, I found myself becoming more aware of a living Christ who could be my personal friend." The friendship partners around Carol were skilled at using God's Word and were not hesitant to use Scripture in their conversations.

As you share your faith, don't hesitate to support what you say with the Bible. Quote from it, and turn to it as an authority for answering questions and dealing with life situations.

- If your international friend has doubts about the authenticity or historical accuracy of the Bible, here are three good books for you to read and research appropriate responses:

    Tell It Well: Communicating Across Cultures by John T. Seamands (Beacon Hill Press).

    How to Give Away Your Faith by Paul E. Little (InterVarsity Press).

    Evidence That Demands a Verdict by Josh McDowell (Thomas Nelson Publishers).

- Tell your international friend about the biblical concept of God. The idea of a personal, all-holy, yet all-loving God may sound strange to your international friend. But we must consider who God is if we are to tell about the importance of what he has done for us.

- Talk with your international friend about the biblical concept of man. World religions and philosophies often portray man in the best possible light. The concept of man as a sinner in willful rebellion against God is difficult for most people to accept. Yet the Bible teaches this harsh truth. As sinners we live in a broken relationship with God; the only way to mend this relationship is by repentance and asking for forgiveness.

- Acquire appropriate literature for you and your international friend to study together. You could offer him or her Scripture portions from a modern English translation such as the *New Living Bible* or the *New International Version* or even a translation into the student's own language. The gospel of Luke may be the best portion to start with, followed by the gospel of John. "Diglot" versions (a bilingual Bible with English and another language) can be extremely helpful. At the appropriate time, you may wish to give the student a complete Bible in his or her own language. Bible translations in almost any language can be purchased from the International Bible Society. For more information, call the IBS Customer Service Department at 1-800-524-1588, or write to International Bible Society, Customer Service Department, P.O. Box 62970, Colorado Springs, CO 80967-2970 or International Students, Incorporated: 1-800-ISI-TEAM.

Rely on the Example of Jesus Christ

Jesus told his disciples, "Let your light shine before men, that they may see your good deeds and praise your Father in heaven" (Matthew 5:16).

Consider the life of Jesus Christ. He met the needs of people everywhere. If they were sick, he reached out and touched them and they were healed. If they were bound up with demons, he touched them and freed them. He met people right where they were at the time.

As you develop a friendship with an international student, he may ask, "Why are you helping me?" An appropriate response is "Because I've experienced Jesus' goodness in my life, and he's told me to show kindness to others."

Our words and our actions should provide natural opportunities to share our faith. As you witness to your international friend, make Jesus central to everything. The life and teachings of Jesus as found in the Bible command great respect around the world. Build your conversation on him. What does your international friend know about Jesus? Does he know what claims Jesus made about himself?

- Use illustrations, stories, and parables as Jesus did to illustrate truth. As we said before, in many cultures this approach is more appreciated than straight logic.
- Focus on the death and resurrection of Jesus. Why did Jesus die, and what is the importance of his resurrection? These two concepts should be the heart of our evangelism. As the apostle Paul confirms, "What I received I passed on to you as of first importance: that Christ died for our sins according to the Scriptures, that He was buried, that He was raised on the third day . . ." (1 Corinthians 15:3-4).
- Explain what Jesus means to you. You are living proof of what Jesus

has done and is doing in the world. The international student in your home may revere a teacher or prophet who died many years ago, but as Christians, we fellowship with a living Savior and Lord who has transformed our lives. Through the power of the Holy Spirit, we are able to abide by the teachings of Jesus and make right decisions about moral standards, race relations, the importance of people over things, and all kinds of issues and situations that touch our daily lives.

Use a Variety of Resources (Don't Go It Alone)

Don't try to be a one-man show. There are all sorts of resources and help available to aid you in telling an international student the Good News.

- *The witness of others*. Introduce your international friend to other Christians who come from different social, economic, and educational backgrounds. Some of these Christians may be facing struggles, yet contact with such people can be a testimony to your friend of the reality of the Christian faith. Often God uses more than one Christian to bring a person to faith in Christ.

- *Prayer*. Offer to pray for the international students you know, especially when they face specific problems. Sometimes this is all the witness you can be to these students. As Christians we know to rely on God to do the work of changing people's hearts.

- *Christian fellowship*. Invite your international friend to join you in attending Christian events and activities, such as Bible studies, church programs, retreats, musical programs—even your own family devotions. Be alert to events planned especially for international students. Be careful to explain to your non-Christian friends the nature and program of the meeting or activity they will be attending.

- *Christian support materials*. There are many good books to share with an international student who is curious or interested in the Christian faith. Be selective in the material you offer, so that it is appropriate to the place your friend is at on his pilgrimage. Here are a few recommended titles to consider:

Mere Christianity by C. S. Lewis (Simon & Schuster).

Basic Christianity by John R. W. Stott (InterVarsity Press).

Knowing God by J. I. Packer (InterVarsity Press).

Can Man Live Without God? by Ravi Zacharias (Word Publishing).

- Scripture portions in the student's native language are always a good place to start. Begin with the Gospel of Luke, followed by the Gospel of John. A bilingual version might be especially helpful.

Understanding World Religions

To talk about spiritual subjects with an international student, you will need to have a basic understanding about their religious background. You don't need to be an expert in world religions to be effective in sharing your faith. As mentioned previously, the best resource for understanding world religions is *The Compact Guide to World Religions* by Dean C. Halverson, General Editor and World Religions Specialist for International Students, Incorporated (Bethany House Publishers). With clear, easy-to-use chapters and concise charts, this book helps you understand the origins, basic beliefs, evangelistic challenges and opportunities of the world's religions. Our next chapter will highlight some specific insights in evangelism for internationals from different backgrounds.

Fran, from the People's Republic of China, has been studying at a university in the Midwest. She regularly attends a Bible study for international students. Recently Fran talked about her American friends saying, "As Christians, they never force or persuade us to become Christians. It is more important for them to share Christ's love with us. As loving representatives, they are patient, tolerant, and friendly. . . . Through Christians, I know what is a Christian's quality, and I feel caring and love from the Church. I am not a Christian, but I want to say, 'I appreciate you, all Christians. I thank Lord Jesus for sending you to help us who need help.' "

Open the Opportunity to Discuss Spiritual Topics

Many times the student begins asking spiritual questions and will open this topic of discussion. However, if the subject never comes into your conversation, you can encourage it by using some of the following questions:

- Where do you consider yourself to be spiritually?
- Do you consider yourself a Muslim (or Buddhist, or Hindu)?

An international student from Turkey gave an interesting answer to this question posed by his friendship partner. He said, "I guess you'd say that, since that's all I've ever known, but I'm very interested in Christianity." It launched an interesting spiritual discussion.

- What are some of the religious practices of your country? Does your family practice these? How about you?
- Would you like to know what Christians believe?
- What do people in your country believe about God? Jesus Christ? The Bible? The concept of sin, etc.? Do you also believe these things?
- Would you like to learn English through using the Bible?
- Do you have a Bible? Would you like one? I could get one for you. Would you like it in English or your language?
- What are the main differences you see between your religion and Christianity?
- Would you like to learn more about God and our Christian culture?

Share Your Spiritual Journey

One of the most non-offensive tools for sharing your faith in Jesus Christ is your own personal testimony. As you share your own spiritual journey with an international student, he or she can learn from your experience, and it will open doors of conversation to further spiritual discussions.

Maybe it's been years since you've told anyone about your spiritual journey. Take a few minutes to consider these questions:

- What was your life like before you became a Christian?
- How did you become a Christian?
- How has your life changed since becoming a Christian?
- You may want to write a short outline of the points of your life you'd like to cover. Practice giving your testimony to a close friend. Before you give it to your international friend, ask your Christian friend to monitor your language. As Christians, we tend to fall into our church jargon: "born again," "saved," etc. Look for ways to express yourself without using these buzz words.

Also, by practicing ahead of time, you will gain some confidence and be able to create a target for discussion afterward. Make sure you stick to the point. Don't wander with your storytelling. For example, can you list three benefits added to your life through following Jesus Christ? These benefits would be the major points to stress for the third question: How has your life changed since becoming a Christian?

Use *Knowing God Personally*

When it comes to tracts and tools for evangelism, there are a variety that people use: *Steps to Peace With God* or the *Four Spiritual Laws* are common ones. International Students, Incorporated has created a special tool called *Knowing God Personally*. It is designed for youth, to emphasize relationships, and was written for international students. The tract is simple to use and covers everything that a student needs to know. It emphasizes what the Bible says about Jesus Christ, and can be read together. The student can then take it home for reading again and again. This resource is available directly from ISI (see resource list in Appendix A). It is reproduced at the back of this book.

How to Use *Knowing God Personally*

Pre-evangelism: You can read through *Knowing God Personally* with your international friend, explaining how Christ gave his life for our sins and how we can know him personally. Leave the booklet with the student to reflect on and to share his or her response with you later.

Evangelism: Read through *Knowing God Personally*, explaining any area that needs further detail. Use your Bible, if available, to amplify each point. Share your own testimony as well, using *Knowing God Personally* as a guide for your discussion.

Be sure to address the questions regarding one's personal salvation and ask if he or she is ready to make a commitment. If so, share a similar prayer out loud. Verbalizing the prayer aloud brings the student to a decision point that he or she may not follow through with should you ask him or her to pray silently. It also helps you measure the sincerity of his or her decision.

If the international student has trouble praying the prayer out loud, simply pray the prayer together, or allow him or her to repeat it after you, using his or her own words. Explain to the student that prayer is simply talking to God.

Follow-up to the Commitment: Never assume that any explanation of the Gospel is so easily understood that one comprehends it in a single review. One of the largest evangelistic denominations in North America indicates that the average North American receives twenty-four different presentations of the Gospel before responding.

The international student may require even more. Therefore, after a commitment is made, it is appropriate to review *Knowing God Personally* again. In this way, you can answer his or her questions, emphasize the promises of God, and encourage the student in his or her walk with him. Students can also learn to share their faith in Christ with others, building upon the tool with their own testimony and knowledge of the Scriptures, regardless of how rudimentary their grasp is. The end result is that they are more likely to lead others to him.

Knowing God Personally is a tool that anyone can use for pre-evangelism, evangelism, or commitment follow-up. Study its pages until you feel completely comfortable in sharing your faith and using this tool.

Reasons for Hesitancy in Response

Be sensitive to how your international friend responds as you share your faith. There are a multitude of reasons that make it difficult for your international friend to openly profess faith in Jesus Christ. Try to understand his or her situation, and recognize that there could be a variety of factors that keep the student from making a public commitment to Christ.

- If your friend forsakes his or her family's traditional religion, he or she may face family pressure, possible loss of job or financial support, and perhaps even disinheritance.
- Your friend may face severe persecution, even death, if he or she returns home as a Christian to a country that prohibits Christianity.
- If your friend becomes a Christian and returns to a country where Christianity is held in low regard, he or she may have to discard political or leadership ambitions.
- Your friend may be preoccupied with his or her own goals and academic achievements and not want to consider spiritual needs at this time.
- International students often view Christianity as a Western religion.
- He or she may find it difficult to separate Christianity from political structures and democracy.

- Your friend may be disillusioned by prior contact with either nominal or overly aggressive Christians.
- Friends or nationals who studied in the United States previously may have "warned" him or her about Christianity.

Issues Often Raised by International Students

There are some common questions international students ask in the area of spirituality. Some basic answers and responses are included in the next few sections. As you consider your response to these issues, think about the example of Jesus as he dealt with tough issues and questions. He did not always answer the question he was asked, and sometimes he asked counter-questions. He often looked to the motive of the questioner. And he relied on the Scriptures for the most appropriate answers.

Before you attempt to answer an international student's questions, consider the questioner. Some people are not ready for answers, or at least, answers in detail. Some questions or issues are not genuine. Perhaps the person only wants to cause trouble or obscure the important issues. We must be cautious and prayerful in our responses.

Keep in mind that you will not be able to answer every question—don't try. Don't hesitate to consult the expertise of other authoritative sources, such as your pastor, Christian writers, or other sincere Christians.

Issues and Possible Responses

Issue: The Bible is full of mistakes and contradictions. The Bible has been changed and corrupted.

Response: You might ask whether this understanding comes from your international friend's personal study or if it's an impression he or she has received from somewhere else. Offer to lend your friend material that gives evidence for the reliability of the Scriptures. Encourage him or her to read the Bible. Books such as *Evidence That Demands a Verdict (Volumes 1 and 2)* by Josh McDowell are excellent in this area.

Issue: Christianity is too narrow and exclusive. All religions are really the same and equally valid.

Response: You could answer, "In science, mathematics, and other fields of learning, truth is narrow and follows specific rules and often exclusive logic. Why should Christianity be different?" Jesus taught that spiritual truth is narrow. Jesus said that he is the only way to God and his Word alone is our authority.

Issue: What happens to those who have never heard about Jesus? Or those who are morally good but not Christians?

Response: The Bible teaches that all people are lost and need salvation, regardless of time, location, or apparent moral goodness. The Bible also says, "For all have sinned and fall short of the glory of God" (Romans 3:23). And yet we understand from the Bible that:

- God loved us enough to send Jesus to save us (John 3:16-21).
- God's plan for our salvation has existed since the beginning (Isaiah 9:2,6-7 and John 1:10-14).
- God's plan for salvation is simple (1 John 1:8-9).
- We must have faith to please God (Hebrews 11:6).
- God deals with mankind justly (Genesis 18:25).
- God will not let man ignore him (Romans 1:18-32).
- The person who follows God will be blessed (Psalm 1:1-3).

Issue: There are so many Christian churches, denominations, and groups. Which one, if any, is the right one?

Response: You could answer, "All people who have made Jesus Lord and Savior of their lives are—under the authority of the Bible—one in him." You may deem it appropriate to explain that throughout history Christians have not always agreed with each other on certain points; such discord may reflect cultural tradition, unclear interpretation of the Bible, and even error and conflict between believers. Also, you may explain that there are many churches and religions in the United States because of the laws allowing religious freedom. Historically, many people (with differing beliefs) came to the United States seeking religious freedom.

Issue: How can God be three and one at the same time? How can God have a Son?

Response: This kind of question can be a good lesson for your international friend, in that you may not be able to fully or clearly give an answer. How can finite human beings understand the nature of an infinite God? Not all areas of God's truth, as revealed in the Bible, are easy to understand. That's why we have faith, trusting God for some of these answers. You may want to give your international friend (or study with him or her) the excellent aforementioned book *The Compact Guide to*

World Religions by Dean C. Halverson. Note that the last two chapters deal concisely with Jesus as God and the Bible as God's Word.

Jesus Video (and Study Guide)

Robert and Cynthia had built a good relationship with Zhang, a professor in his fifties from mainland China. Since Zhang had a family of his own back in China, he enjoyed the casual visits with Robert, Cynthia, and their children. He especially enjoyed the long talks with Robert as they shared about different cultures and views on life. Zhang even pulled books from Robert's bookshelf about China or Christianity and then asked questions.

One night Robert asked Zhang and another professor to visit his church and see a movie about the life of Jesus Christ. As they sat together on either side of Robert, their eyes were riveted to the unfolding story. During the crucifixion scene, Robert was a bit shocked when Zhang put his hand on top of Robert's. As Robert turned in his surprise, he saw tears streaming down Professor Zhang's face. Then he said, "This is too wonderful. I did not know that God did this for me."

Months later, Robert and Cynthia took Zhang to the airport to catch his plane back to China. As Zhang entered the jetway to board the plane, he paused, turned around, and came back to Robert. He hugged Robert with a very uncharacteristic show of affection, saying, "Please do not forget me. Please pray for me and my family." Millions of people around the world have made a personal commitment to Jesus Christ after watching the *Jesus* video. It is available in nearly every language through ISI (see Appendix A). Based on the Gospel of Luke, this film is an excellent tool for international students. Ask your friend if he or she would like to view this video with you.

Before viewing the film:

Before a student can understand the person of Jesus Christ, he or she must first understand who we believe God to be. Take the student to Genesis 1:1. From this passage, we can see that God existed before the world, is powerful, a creator, a personal God. Looking at Genesis 3, tell the student about how sin entered the world and about God's promise to deal with Satan. Genesis 12 gives God's promise to bless all nations.

Discuss the prophecies about the coming of Jesus Christ. These show that God's plan was in operation throughout history. Read with the student Acts 17:22-34. In these verses, Paul explains to the Athenians the identity of the Unknown God. Let your international friend read verses 24-31, after explaining the context to him or her. After the student understands the concept of the Christian God, explain the concept of sin that separated us from God, and thus, the need for the Savior, Jesus Christ. After you have laid this groundwork with the student, you are ready to watch the video on the life of Jesus Christ.

A discussion and study guide is available with the film from ISI (see Appendix A). This guide provides helpful questions to direct your discussion about the video after you have viewed it together.

Because the *Jesus* video is available in many languages, you may want to give the student a copy of the video in his or her native language. This video is especially appropriate as a Christmas gift or as gift when he or she is returning home. It can be purchased in a format that is compatible with the foreign video system.

Throw a Discussion Party

Bill and Mary were involved with many international students from their local university. Every Friday evening they hosted a small group dinner with some of the students and discussed questions the students had about the Bible and the Christian faith.

One evening they were watching a clip from the *Jesus* film and discussing the crucifixion of Jesus Christ. After the discussion, Shinji, a new attender to the discussion group from Japan, sat down next to Bill.

"Bill, tonight is first time I ever see a Bible. Can I ask you a question? We talk about God. God this and God that. This is very interesting to me. Can you tell me, who is God? I never hear of him in my country when I am growing up. I like to know more."

ISI has a guide for hosting a discussion party, called *Let's Talk About It* (see Appendix A). The majority of the contents of this publication are summarized in the following pages.

A discussion party involves several families who meet to discuss life and issues about God. The forum of a discussion allows students to openly express their views. You will be amazed at how the truth of God comes to light during these discussion times. This format allows students to talk about interesting topics that might not otherwise be brought into routine conversation. These parties provide a relaxed atmosphere where internationals can have fun with American Christians without fear of rejection, hostility, or harmful argument.

The purpose of such a gathering is to help friendship partners and international students become better acquainted and communicate on deeper levels. These gatherings will crystallize each participant's thinking regarding his or her beliefs about issues. Also, it gives internationals a clearer understanding of Christianity by experiencing Christian love and acceptance, seeing the validity of biblical truth, and beginning to grasp the implications of biblical Christianity.

The ideal use for this program involves five discussion parties, each lasting two hours. The first two weeks are orientation sessions for the friendship partners, while during the last three weeks, both the friendship partners and internationals participate.

During the first session for the friendship partners, they get acquainted, discuss the overview of a discussion party, learn how to invite students, and pray for the results of the parties. Also during this first session, the friendship partners choose a topic for the discussion parties. Some of the possibilities are included below. In the second session, the friendship partners discuss the process of evangelism and role play a potential discussion, and again pray for the series of parties. The process of evangelism with international students has been covered elsewhere in this book (such as attitudes about successful evangelism—it's a process and not a one-time event). After each of the three discussions with international students, the friendship partner and an international student meet for one-on-one discussion.

Guidelines for Effective Discussion

These guidelines form the basic ground rules for the discussion parties. They are important because they will set the tone for the entire sessions and the comfort level of every participant.

- Help the internationals feel accepted, and encourage them to freely share their opinions. Let them know their opinions will be accepted.
- Be enthusiastic and friendly.
- Contribute freely to the discussion, but don't do all the talking.
- Wait until an individual is finished sharing his or her point of view before responding.

- Be gentle in responding to someone's point of view. Never argue.
- Don't play the "devil's advocate" or pose as a non-Christian.
- Internationals from some cultures may be hesitant to speak out in a group or in the presence of their host or hostess. Be sensitive to this, and try to "draw out" more reserved participants.
- Stick to the topic; don't go off on a tangent.
- Don't be afraid to clearly present a biblical viewpoint on the issue. However, avoid stifling the discussion with "cut-and-dried" answers. If others feel that you are not open to truly hearing their ideas because you already have "the answer," they will not respond as openly and the discussion will deteriorate.
- Articulate your answers carefully. Avoid slang words, idioms, and Christian jargon.
- Be sure the internationals leave the discussion party knowing that you like them for who they are.

After the discussion party: Usually the most meaningful interaction will take place after the party is over. The discussion itself is the vehicle for this interaction. Here are some helpful hints to make this informal time more profitable:

- Avoid huddling with other hosts and thereby excluding international guests with whom you could interact.
- Be sensitive to persons standing alone or those with apparent needs. Be friendly and relaxed.
- Continue the dialogue on a one-on-one basis, or at least in very small groups. Start the conversation with something like: "I didn't get to hear your impression of the discussion. What do you think?" or "Your comment on _____ was very interesting."
- Ask an international with whom you have a good relationship what he or she thought about the discussion time. And remember, it is generally unwise to invite someone to accept Christ at a discussion party. Trust God and be patient for a future opportunity to share your personal faith and the Good News of Christ with your international friend.

Selecting a Discussion Topic

When choosing a topic for the discussion party, it should be

- interesting to the participants;

- important to the participants;
- within the knowledge and experience of the group;
- international in scope.

Specific topics related to ethics, philosophy, love, marriage, politics, and religion are usually of great interest to international students and friendship partners. A list of some topics and actual questions are furnished in Appendix B. You may want to talk with some international students and get their suggestions about topics of current interest. Or select a topic for the first discussion party, then allow the participants to select the topics for the subsequent sessions.

Every participant in the discussion party should know the topic well in advance of the meeting. Use the first topic in your invitation to international students, then at the conclusion of the first session, agree on the next topic. Present the topic informally, yet with enthusiasm. For example, "I've been thinking about a topic I think everyone would enjoy discussing. . . ." Every participant should be given the opportunity to research and prepare for discussion on the topic.

Sometimes a good topic is suggested but the scope is too narrow for an international discussion. For example, one student might say, "It seems that America has few friends in the Middle East. I would like to discuss America's role in the Middle East." If used for discussion, this question could lead to a sectarian debate that might not be productive. To expand this question so that everyone could participate, the moderator might say, "Because we have so many nations represented here tonight, we may want to rephrase your question to say something like, 'What attitudes and actions do you think are being expressed by the developing nations and industrialized nations in regard to the Middle East?' "

Prepare for the Discussion

After the topic is selected, secure information pertinent to the discussion by reading relevant books and articles. Discover good quotations or current news events that relate to the topic, or interview people familiar with the issues you hope to discuss. Then organize your information to assist in guiding the discussion. What issues should be discussed? What are possible solutions to at least some of the problems related to the issue?

Formulating questions: Each discussion topic should be approached with the attitude of a co-learner rather than a scholar. Don't appear to have all the answers from your preparation. You don't. Clearly define the issues you hope to discuss, and develop appropriate questions. Questions, not statements, enhance discussions. Here are some guidelines to creating good questions:

- Limit the questions to a single topic. Briefly touching on several topics in a single discussion party will only confuse group members. Let the participants cover one topic as completely as they desire so they can gain a good understanding of their own thinking and the thinking of others. Be careful that the discussion does not become a dialogue between only two or three participants.
- Use "open-ended" questions—that is, questions that lead to a variety of responses. Try not to ask questions that can be answered by a simple yes or no. A monosyllabic answer in itself will not stimulate discussion. Ask participants to explain their answers.
- Avoid questions that assume a certain answer will be given.
- Ask questions that will lead from facts to opinions to personal application as the discussion progresses.
- Make your questions clear and to the point. Keep in mind that some of the internationals may not understand slang, puns, or irony.
- Formulate enough questions to keep the discussion party going for about an hour. You may want to have a few optional questions on hand in case the discussion begins to lag. Be sensitive to the group's needs, and guide the group members out of arguments or diversions.
- Avoid any ambiguous wording in your questions.

Prepare the Place for Discussion

The environment for your discussion party will make a difference as to its success. A home with a large living room, den, or recreational area is the most comfortable environment. The host or hostess should be responsible for preparations. If you have a larger group, try to find a comfortable meeting room in a dorm, the student union, or a campus church. If possible, appoint someone besides yourself to be responsible for the preparations and to act as a "host" or "hostess." Here are some things that the host or hostess should keep in mind:

- Provide a comfortable, informal atmosphere—one that allows for relaxation, but not sleep! Keep your discussion group with no less than six and no more than twelve for the best discussion.
- During the initial get-acquainted time and after the discussion, provide some simple yet appealing refreshments such as crackers, fruit, and/or vegetables with dip, as well as sweets.
- Provide name tags for all participants; use a felt-tip marker that shows clearly and legibly. You may want to ask the international students to write their home countries as well as their preferred names on the tags.
- Arrange the seating so that all members can see one another. A circle is best.
- Provide adequate lighting so that it is easy to see others, and adequate ventilation to keep the discussion lively.

Inviting Internationals to a Discussion Party

As a friendship partner, you are responsible for inviting your international friend to the discussion party series. If possible, invite at least one of his international friends to join you at the party. The discussion party is most effective when the ratio of internationals to Americans is about two to one.

Here are some suggestions for inviting students:

- Invite them about two weeks in advance. Follow up the initial invitation with a reminder phone call about five days in advance.
- Describe the evening as a party where people will discuss topics of interest to internationals. You may mention, if it is appropriate, that the evening is sponsored by a church, but assure them that no pressure will be exerted on them.
- Arrange to pick up the internationals and take them to the discussion party. Consider inviting them to dinner before the party. The dinner might give you an opportunity to establish rapport before the party begins.

Guidelines for the Moderator

Every discussion party needs a moderator to guide the group conversation. If you have taken the role of moderator, there are some additional guidelines to keep in mind.

During the first meeting of the discussion party, make sure everyone agrees to two clear promises:

1. The group discussion time will be limited to exactly one hour.

2. All opinions, ideas, and beliefs will be accepted and appreciated.

Your role as the moderator is to present each topic to be discussed and moderate the discussion. You will not be giving a lecture. Instead, your task is to facilitate participation from every member of the group. Participation can be:

- *Spontaneous*. The simplest and perhaps most comfortable way to direct a discussion is to allow participants to speak freely. However, if the group members are not well acquainted, or not experienced in discussion, some moderation may be necessary.

- *By your recognition*. Having group members raise their hands and speak only when you recognize them helps control objectivity during emotional or controversial times when several participants want to talk at once.

- *By your directed questioning*. If the discussion is lagging, or if a few vocal members are dominating the discussion, you may need to direct specific questions to specific individuals. Simply say something like, "Lee, what do *you* think about this issue?"

You will discover that each of these methods comes into use during a discussion evening. If the discussion begins slowly, you may have to ask specific individuals questions. Once the discussion picks up, participants will feel free to speak up. During an emotional time, you may say, "Why don't we speak one at a time. Ali, would you like to go first?"

Here are some additional points to keep in mind:

- Be patient and be a good listener.
- Encourage and compliment every sincere contribution.
- Be unobtrusive. Don't force your ideas on others. Be genuinely interested in what other people say.
- Be sensitive to the group's dynamics. If discussion stalls, try to motivate participation by rephrasing questions or making them more specific.
- Take time to coordinate and integrate opinions. Follow up with questions or statements which will help the participants clarify their opinions and reach conclusions.

- From time to time, briefly summarize the group's conclusions. Try to keep others from summarizing the conclusions and forcing their personal opinions on the group.
- Handle emotional outbursts by allowing momentary silence and having the emotional individual repeat themselves after they become more calm. Try to prevent others from reacting too strongly to such a situation. Although some tension and controversy stimulates thinking, do your best to maintain a relaxed discussion atmosphere at all times.

At the end of the discussion party, summarize the basic issues discussed and the group's conclusions. Remember, the purpose of the discussion party is to help participants crystallize their thinking, not to confuse them. Tactfully present some Christian perspectives to leave the participants with "food for thought" that will stimulate one-on-one discussions following the group session. Include the Christians present in the after-discussion interaction.

Announce the topic for the next discussion party. Present a few thought-provoking questions that will give the participants a taste of the next discussion. Make them want to come back. Thank the group for coming and announce the time and place of the next discussion party.

As soon as the discussion party ends, make sure the friendship partners mingle with the international students. Participate in these informal discussion times, making yourself available to answer any questions from international students. Again, make sure that no international is "forced" to discuss Christianity. Being a friend is the most important aspect, and times to discuss Jesus and the Bible will occur naturally at a later time.

A Variety of Tools

Sharing your personal testimony, the *Knowing God Personally* tract, discussion parties, and the *Jesus* video are tools to help an international learn how to have a personal relationship with God through Jesus Christ. Remember, the most important things are

- to establish a loving relationship with the international student for Christ's sake—agape love with no personal strings attached.
- to give the student an opportunity to ask questions and receive information about spiritual life in a nonthreatening situation.

- to use appropriate tools (tracts, Bible studies, videos, discussion guides).

Apply What You Have Learned

1. Pray for the international students you know.
2. Review the various methods of sharing your faith. Which have you attempted? What approach is the most comfortable for you? Which approach would cause you to grow in your spiritual relationship?
3. Write down three or four ways you can minister through your life to your student with acts of love. These actions will open the door for you to possibly share your faith with him or her.
4. Get copies of *Knowing God Personally*, and go over it with a friend so you will be comfortable sharing it with your international friend.
5. Choose one book on sharing your faith or answering spiritual questions that may be asked by your student. Commit to reading two books over the next three months.
6. Plan a fun time—a discussion party with several friends and students.
7. Follow up with any students who attend the discussion party, especially regarding any questions that might not have been fully answered.

EIGHT

Sorting the Luggage

"Jesus answered, 'I am the way and the truth and the life.
No one comes to the Father except through me.'"

John 14:6

Karen was worried. In a few hours, she would meet an international student from the People's Republic of China for the first time. She had studied a map of China and looked through some basic reference information. Unfortunately there was little information about the spiritual climate of China or other necessary background about her new Chinese friend. Her problem was, what was she going to say?

Unless we learn about the spiritual differences between each religion or background, such as Arabic, Japanese, Chinese, or African, it is difficult to know how to help our new friends in the areas of spirituality. This chapter will help you sort through the various religious backgrounds and provide some historical framework and key areas for preparation. It will help you as you relate to students from their particular orientation. Also you will want to return to these sections immediately prior to meeting an international student who may be a Muslim or from mainland China. Preparation will enhance your relationship and increase your effectiveness in leading your friend toward a personal relationship with Jesus Christ.

As we have mentioned before, the most authoritative and easy to use source of information about religions is *The Compact Guide to World Religions*. This book covers the material in greater detail. What we will do here is give you some brief information about Islamic, Chinese, Japanese, and African cultures.

Specialized Approaches for Students From Particular Backgrounds

ISLAM

There are over 500,000 international students, and an estimated 77,000 of them are from the Islamic areas of the world, representing some 40 countries, of which 80 to 100 percent are Muslim. These students are part of a worldwide population of more than 850 million Muslims, clearly the second largest religion in the world. The number of American Muslims is estimated to be about five million.

Because most Muslims have had as little contact with Christianity as Christians have had with Islam, there are some unique opportunities to share Christ with these international students. In fact, many Muslims come from countries where no Christian witness or Bible teaching has been permitted for centuries.

As sensitive Christians, we know we cannot force our beliefs on our Muslim friends. Yet we desire to share the hope within us. There is no easy formula for witnessing to a Muslim. The key principles are:

1. Be a true friend.
2. Live your faith boldly.
3. Use the Word of God.

Indeed, people of the Islamic faith represent a variety of cultures and subgroups from many nations. Therefore, we must follow the example of Jesus, who never dealt with any two individuals the same way. He simply said, "Come, follow me, and I will make you fishers of men."

Understanding Cultural Expectations

To befriend a Muslim, it's important to understand the cultural expectations. Here are several key areas:

Friendship

People in every society value friendship, but they express it in different ways. For most Muslims, friendship involves an investment of time and effort: to be together, relate to one another, share food, talk, and much more. Muslims may have only a few friends, but they are usually willing to commit their lives, wealth, and good names to their friends.

Americans have difficulty meeting such a standard; in fact, the complaint of many Muslims is that most Americans seem superficial in their expression of friendship. We need to be conscious of our Muslim friend's expectations and be the best friend we can be. In Muslim countries, most friendships are between people of the same sex. Close relationships between people of the opposite sex who are not immediate relatives are unusual. Both you and the Muslim students you meet will probably be more comfortable in relationships between the same sex.

Hospitality

Hospitality is a way of life for Muslims. If you are invited into the home of a Muslim family, they will almost always offer food and drink, no matter how brief your visit. Your friends will look for the same hospitality from you. When you invite them into your home, remember to offer refreshments or share a meal. You don't have to be elaborate in your hospitality, but simply offer whatever is available, such as fresh fruit, coffee, or tea.

Devout Muslims do not eat pork or drink any alcoholic beverages. However, many Muslims learn to drink alcohol after coming to the United States and often assume all Americans drink. Don't be surprised if your Muslim friends offer alcohol as a part of their hospitality.

Conversation

Conversation and the exchange of ideas will be more important to your Muslim friends than activities or meetings. You don't always have to do something special. Just invite them over; they may savor the opportunity to relax and "feel at home."

You may find that you and your Muslim friend hold opposing views on important issues, enough to get into an argument. While arguments can be counterproductive, many Muslims enjoy a good argument. It is not uncommon to see students from a Muslim country hotly debate a subject one minute and warmly embrace the next. You need not always be in agreement with your Muslim friend to maintain the friendship. As a Christian, you will not agree with many of the beliefs your Muslim friend holds, but don't worry about it. Of course, you should listen to and try to understand what your friend is saying before giving a response. Learn to disagree amiably. In many Muslim countries, disagreements are often a way to test friendships.

Time and Obligations

To most Americans, time is extremely important. We tend to keep tight schedules for ourselves and expect an appointment will be kept within a few minutes or so of the designated time. Much of the rest of the world, including the Muslim world, may not observe such guidelines. When making an appointment with your Muslim friend, discuss your expectations. Remind your friend of the engagement, learn to be patient, and try to be sensitive to his or her expectations. For example, if you are invited to a Muslim home for a meal, your host may wish to socialize with you before eating. You may want to do the same when you invite Muslim friends to your home.

Sometimes you may feel "stood up" by your Muslim friend. There might be several explanations for this. Your friend perhaps neglected to write a reminder note and simply forgot the invitation. Or he may have had unexpected visitors; in an effort to attend to these guests (which is an important social obligation in Islamic cultures), your friend may have overlooked his prior commitment to you. If you have been disappointed by a Muslim friend, don't give up. Be understanding and try again.

Witness by Action and Word

Jesus is our example. As you develop friendships with Muslim students, they may ask, "Why are you helping me?" An appropriate response is "Because I've experienced God's goodness in my life, and he's told me to show kindness to others." We should model Jesus. He met the needs of others—physically, emotionally, and spiritually . . . with no personal strings attached. Our Muslim friends will be watching closely. We must be available as a daily witness of God's love in our lives. Our words and actions should provide natural opportunities to share our faith.

Understanding Islam

Know Your Audience

You don't need to be an expert on the Islamic faith to befriend a Muslim and share your faith with him or her. The Christian who makes an effort to investigate the religious convictions of others, however, is in a better position to communicate what he believes.

Christians sometimes make the mistake of calling Muslims "Mohammedans." But Muslims do not regard the prophet Mohammed the same way as we follow and worship Jesus Christ. Mohammed lived from A.D. 570 to 632, mainly in Mecca and Medina on the Arabian peninsula. He united the Arab peoples and abolished their former polytheism. Muslims don't believe Mohammed to be divine, but consider him to be "God's Messenger," last in the series of great prophets—including Abraham, Moses, and Jesus. It is neither wise nor appropriate for Christians to speak against Mohammed. While we can not call him "The Prophet"— as Muslims do—we ought to show respect for what Mohammed taught his followers.

Religious Practices

"Islam" is an Arabic word meaning "surrender" or "submission." A Muslim is one who is surrendered to God. This slave-like submission is reflected in five ritualistic practices, which are often referred to as the five pillars of Islam. These are:

- *Declaration*: The main tenet of Islamic faith is the declaration that "Allah is one and Mohammed is his prophet."
- *Prayer*: Muslims participate in five prayer sessions at specified intervals throughout the day, which require prostration in the direction of Mecca and recitation of verses from the Qur'an (or Koran).
- *Fasting*: Every year devout Muslims will keep a fast during the month of Ramadan, in which the believer refrains from food and drink between sunrise and sunset.
- *Tithe*: Muslims give a charitable contribution of 2.5 (1/40th) percent of their total income to the poor, homeless, needy, and to those who fight for Islam.
- *The Holy Land*: Most Muslims hold to the once-in-a-lifetime dream of going on a pilgrimage (called the Hajj) to the birthplace of Islam, the holy city of Mecca, in Saudi Arabia.

Devout Muslims will do their best to observe all of these dictums, but you will find great variation in the dedication and observance among people of Islamic faith, especially among those living away from home here in the West.

The Qur'an

Muslims believe that the Qur'an (Koran), the Islamic scripture, was directly dictated by God through the angel Gabriel to Mohammed. Although Muslims respect the Bible, they value the Qur'an above the Bible as the last and final revelation of God. The Qur'an is not an easy book to translate because of its Arabic, poetic content. Orthodox Muslims declare that the Qur'an cannot be translated and ought to be studied in Arabic, since "that is the language in which God revealed it." This book is about two-thirds the length of the New Testament and contains 114 Suras (chapters) that are arranged according to length (from the longest to shortest) rather than chronologically.

Because of a traditional belief that Mohammed was uneducated and illiterate and yet able to utter the sayings for the holy book, the Qur'an is often called "the miracle of Mohammed." The Qur'an is the supreme validation of the Islam faith. The public recitation of the Qur'an in Arabic is extremely important and highly valued among Muslims.

Islam: A Way of Life

More than Mohammed, the Qur'an, or a stringent set of beliefs, Islam is a way of life. In Muslim societies, Islam encompasses cultural, economic, political, and social as well as religious dimensions. The psychological impact of growing up in such a society cannot be minimized.

When Muslims encounter another religion with different and often contradictory ideas, it can be quite threatening. And yet, the Qur'an teaches that Muslims should respect the "people of the Book," that is, Jews and Christians who follow the Bible and worship the one true God.

Jesus in Islam

Muslims have a high regard for Jesus. In the Qur'an, Jesus is called "the Word of God" (Sura 3:45) and "the Spirit of God" (Sura 4:171). The holy book presents Jesus as one of the great prophets; he is even called "Messiah." Also, Jesus is declared to have been born of the Virgin Mary and to have lived a sinless life (Sura 19:19). He accomplished many wonderful miracles, such as giving sight to the blind, healing lepers, and raising the dead to life (Sura 3:49). According to tradition, Jesus will return again to earth—to establish Islam throughout the world.

But devout Muslims are adamant in denying that Jesus is the "Son of God" or "Savior." In fact, in the Islamic faith, to equate anyone with Allah (or God) is blasphemy, the unforgivable sin. The Qur'an seems to indicate (in Sura 4:156-158) that Jesus was not crucified; instead, God spared him from the cross, taking him to heaven, and had someone else die in Jesus' place. The book, however, is not entirely clear on the subject. (See also Sura 19:33).

Being an Effective Witness to Muslims

The Right Approach

Your Muslim friend will not feel free to ask questions or show any interest in Christianity if other Muslims are present. Your best opportunities for witnessing to Muslim students, therefore, will be on an individual basis.

Identify Beliefs

Before you share Christianity with a Muslim, find out what he or she actually believes—which may or may not be orthodox Islam. Ask questions such as:

- What is the meaning of life?
- Is there a God? Can we know Him?
- What is the nature of man? If man is basically good, why does he often behave so badly?
- Is there life after death?

These questions may help draw your Muslim friends out to share their true beliefs rather than what they have been taught or heard others say.

Discuss Who God Is

Muslims have 99 names for God, most of which concur with the teachings of the Bible. However, the concept of a holy, loving God is not emphasized in Islam, especially in terms of God loving sinners. Share with Muslim students how Christianity teaches that God is our loving Father, and how his care and personal concern affect you personally.

Emphasize Jesus

You may find it helpful to use the Muslim teachings about Jesus as a starting point for a discussion about your faith. For example, you could ask your friend, "When the Qur'an refers to Jesus as the Word of God, what does that suggest to you?"

You will need to emphasize what the Bible says about the life and teachings of Jesus. The Qur'an emphasizes the keeping of rules and regulations that are rather rigid, inflexible, and legalistic. Jesus, on the other hand, gives us freedom from the curse of the law and grace to live righteously in Him. Share with your Muslim friend how you apply the teachings of Jesus to your everyday life.

Use God's Word

As you share your faith, support what you say with the Bible. Quote from it and turn to it as an authority for answering questions and dealing with life situations. Be careful how you physically use your Bible, because how and where a "holy book" is placed says a lot to a Muslim. For example, Muslims always keep the Qur'an in a high place in order to show reverence to their "holy book." In the same respect, you should never place the Bible beneath you, such as under your chair, because this displays an irreverent attitude to Muslims.

Suggest that your Muslim friend read appropriate portions of the Bible, such as the gospel of Luke, followed by the gospel of John. Be prepared to take time to discuss with your friend the exact meaning of the introductory verses of John's gospel.

You will find it helpful to use a modern English translation of the Bible, such as the New International Version, or the New Living Translation Bible, or the Contemporary English Version, or even a translation into the student's own language.

Use the Witness of Others

Invite your Muslim friend to join you in attending Christian events and activities such as Bible studies, church programs, retreats, musical programs—even your own family devotions. Be alert to events planned especially for international students. The combined Christian testimony of yourself and others can be an effective instrument for demonstrating the reality of God in believers' lives.

Never pressure your Muslim friend to go to these activities, and be careful to explain the nature and program of the meeting or activity.

CHINESE

Thousands of students from mainland China are studying in the United States. To effectively reach these students for Jesus Christ, there is a great deal we can learn about the history, culture, and people that will increase the effectiveness of our efforts to share Christ.[1]

Understanding the Chinese Student

Internal Glimpses of Your Friend

Most Chinese students reflect a cultural identity that is a mixture of ancient Confucianism and modern communism. The teachings of Confucius, or Kong Fu-zi (551–479 B.C.), have deeply influenced China for more than twenty-five centuries. Above all else, Confucius emphasized the need for an equitable social order. Confucianism teaches the Chinese to value social relationships, to live proper lives of respect and courtesy toward others, and the denial of self for the good of all. This goes along with Confucius' belief that human nature is basically good but becomes disordered and crippled by a poor environment, such as under the leadership of a weak or corrupt government.

Marxism's ideals regarding human nature and the value of mankind are quite similar to Confucianism. This may explain how easily these two philosophical approaches coexist in many Chinese people. In a sense, Confucianism cleared the way spiritually for communism's temporary success in China. While some Chinese students may now disparage communism, they may be confusing their distaste for this philosophy with their distaste for China's government. In reality, these students still hold to the fundamental principles of communism and will rebuke the teachings of Christianity. That may explain why some Chinese want to adjust and adapt to Western culture, but have difficulty understanding the emphasis placed on individual freedom, religion, and family values.

Basically, Chinese students tend to have three kinds of culture-based resistance to Christianity. First, Chinese intellectuals may resist and reject the Gospel because of concerns that Christianity will destroy traditional Chinese culture. Traditionally, Chinese intelligentsia see Christianity as some kind of superstition or as an inferior foreign philosophy.

Second, many Chinese remember Christianity's historical link with the imperialistic invasion of China in the 1800s. These Chinese might agree with the communist phrase: "Christianity is the running dog of imperialism."

The third form of resistance comes from Marxism's attack against all religion. To the Chinese Marxist, religion only frustrates people's efforts toward happiness. Marxism affirms that man—not a sovereign God—controls his own destiny.

Philosophy

Although many Chinese students may not think of themselves as "communists," in reality their worldview is identical to communism. They will tend to accept certain Marxist doctrines as the only proper way to view the world:

- Human beings create and decide human history.
- Science leads man to truth.
- Religion (especially Christianity) is opium to people.

While many Chinese students will accept these teachings as fact, most know little or nothing about the source, which is Marxism. Very few have even read anything by Karl Marx. What these students know and believe is what the Chinese government has promoted through education and propaganda. Thus, when Chinese students hear about Christianity, their presupposition is that all religions, in essence, are untrue. When Christians explain Christ's pronouncement that he is Truth, they may get one of two responses. The first may be rejection without much consideration. The other may be the questions of a seeker who realizes he has been a victim of indoctrination. Bob sat with the president of the Mainland Chinese Students and Scholars group at an elite university in Southern California. Bob was at the meeting to talk with the Chinese leader about a professional mentoring program that could match Chinese students and scholars with American professionals already established in the same career field. Suddenly, as Bob explained the program, the Chinese scholar interrupted midsentence to say, "You know, all my life in China I am taught that religion is for old people and for foolish people. I do not think this is true. Can you tell me what the Bible teaches?" For the next two hours, the men discussed the claims of Christ.

While Chinese have been indoctrinated with Marxist and atheistic ideology, many have a hunger to know about spiritual things, which have been absent and suppressed in their culture and upbringing. In fact, the mainland Chinese are historically the most open and receptive of all international students to the Gospel and spiritual matters.

Spiritual Experience

In the tradition of Confucianism, many Chinese students have a fundamental problem with two of the major teachings of Christianity: the sinful nature of mankind, and the anticipation of eternal life through belief in Jesus Christ. Central to Confucianism are concepts teaching proper behavior in relationships, both between individuals and under an appropriate government. Thus, Confucius' teachings imply the natural goodness—or at least the natural perfectibility—of humankind.

Also, Confucius' emphasis on reason and practical living leaves little room for discussion about heaven or hell, or even the need for such places. Confucius said, "Without knowing this life, how can I know the life after?" Thus, many Chinese value practicality, concentrating on the here and now, and on cultivating one's own perfectness.

In light of recent history, many Chinese, particularly students in the United States, are experiencing a "crisis of belief." Representing the intellectual community of China, these students and visiting scholars were raised to accept and support communism without exception. They put all of their hope, love, and confidence in this "religion" (though most Chinese would not accept this as a definition for their devotion to communism).

After generations of suffering and persecution for a "new China," the stresses of the Cultural Revolution and the discrediting of Mao's government and supporters, and especially after the Tiananmen Square massacre, many Chinese have become disillusioned with communism and their government. This disillusionment has made some Chinese students hypersensitive about where they can place their faith. Such hypersensitivity carries over into doubt, criticism, and sometimes even discrimination toward other political and religious teachings.

Many Chinese, consciously and unconsciously, are on a spiritual search to find new truth that they hope will help themselves and China's future. This search has often translated into a curiosity about and study of Christianity. China's government, in change, will actually be strengthened through faith.

Many Kinds of Chinese Students

Who Are These Students?

Chinese students in the United States represent the cream of the crop. They have proved their intellectual achievement in their various fields of study. Most Chinese students come to the U.S. for graduate study, usually specializing in the sciences—such as computer science, mathematics, chemistry, physics, biology—and many other natural and social science fields.

One way to understand the many kinds of Chinese students is to consider the different age groups (and backgrounds) of Chinese who study in the U.S. We will divide these students into three major groups: older, middle, and younger.

Older Generation (Ages 40 to 60)

- These "students" (mostly visiting scholars) have the strongest ties with Chinese traditions.
- The people of this generation suffered the most during China's Cultural Revolution.
- These Chinese come to the United States with J-1 visas, usually for limited time periods (one month to two years). More than 95 percent of this group returns home.
- Most of these Chinese have had and will have prominent positions in varied scientific fields in China.
- This group tends to have the poorest adaptability to a new culture, and language skills are a major frustration.
- These Chinese tend to be relatively isolated on their school campuses, and thus more open to genuine friendships.
- They tend to enjoy activities such as potluck meals and tours of the United States. The best ministry results have been in the area of "planting seeds" of knowledge about Christianity, which many will take back to China and share with family and friends. Many others have enjoyed close friendships with American Christians and have returned home as believers.

Middle Generation (Ages 29 to 39)

- These Chinese grew up in the "new China," and were raised under a strict regimen of communistic teachings, primarily atheistic.

- This group includes the children of many prominent Chinese communist leaders.
- From a very young age, these students were politically active, participating in the Red Guard, and were caught up in the ideals of China's Cultural Revolution.
- With the disastrous effects and failure of the Cultural Revolution, many in this group experienced disillusionment and a "crisis of belief."
- These Chinese tend to be ambitious, hardworking, critical, and sometimes selfish. Most have achieved a lifelong dream by going to college and on to graduate school in the United States by their own means.
- About 65 percent of these students come here under a J-1 visa status, and 35 percent under an F-1 visa, basically for long-term graduate study in the United States.
- Many of these students have family with them in the United States. Their children are enrolled in American schools.
- These Chinese have an amazing adaptability to America's culture; most don't want to return to China and hope to settle in the United States permanently.
- These students tend to be critical of Christianity, having many tough questions for which they believe there are no satisfactory answers.
- Ministry to this group requires sensitivity, patience, sincerity, and a willingness to confront tough questions about Christianity. If these Chinese become Christians, they tend to be strong believers, with an eagerness to be discipled and to evangelize others.

Younger Generation (Ages 18 to 28)

- These Chinese may tend to be called "the lucky generation," because they didn't experience many of the hardships brought on by China's Cultural Revolution.
- Many in this group have little or no faith in communism. Instead, they place their faith in science or in their own abilities.
- These Chinese tend to be idealistic, confident, and competitive. They can, however, be naive, with a poor sense of support for what they say they believe.
- Most of these students entered college directly from high school, and they have come to the United States for graduate studies. About ten percent come as undergraduates.

- About half of these students hold J-1 visas, and half hold F-1 visas. Many plan to stay in the U.S. permanently.
- Some are here with their spouses, and a small percentage of these spouses are part- or full-time students themselves.
- Effective ministry approaches with these students include group activities and conferences, where presentations of the Gospel can challenge and correct their presuppositions about Christianity.

Being an Effective Christian with Chinese Students

First Be a Friend

America's "fast" approach to food, entertainment, and even friendship doesn't translate well to the Chinese. They don't consider "acquaintances" as "friends." To most Chinese students, friendship is the result of time and patience, which produces mutual trust. Friendship is also the willingness to sacrifice one's own interests to meet the other's needs.

For example, friends show a sincere interest in each other, asking questions such as: "How are you really doing?" Friends wait for a response. In befriending Chinese students, find out about their personal lives and involve them in yours. Invite them over for meals; introduce them to your friends.

Chinese students in the United States tend to be lonely. Externally, they suffer loneliness because of separation from family, language difficulties, cross-cultural frustrations, financial burdens, and sometimes the insensitivity and inattention of others. Internally, Chinese students may have problems getting along with one another, often because of a cultural tradition of isolation and the fear of persecution from others, especially their government.

Live Out the Christian Life

One impression some Chinese students have about Americans, particularly Christians, is that they have "big mouths but small hands." To the Chinese it seems that Christians are very good at talking about their faith, but their actions fail to demonstrate it.

One Chinese student related his experience with Christians: "Christians don't do what they say every day. My car was stuck in the snow just in front of a church last Sunday. Although many people carrying Bibles saw me, no one stopped to give me a hand. It seemed to me they were more concerned to get into the church on time."

In Chinese culture, action is more important than words. In fact, Chinese people traditionally regard a person who talks too much as untrustworthy. It might be said that the Chinese prefer "down-to-earth" people. In light of this, your Chinese friend may be slow to respond to the Gospel. Your response must be to "walk the talk," live what you believe.

It's been said that when it comes to the Gospel of Jesus Christ, people don't care how much you know until they know how much you care. One woman from Taiwan wanted to be involved in the ISI English class, but she could not make the Sunday morning meetings. Knowing her disappointment, ISI volunteer Brenda Korsten took the English class to her, meeting her every Wednesday on campus to go over her vocabulary words. Each Friday another volunteer, David Palmer, met with her to discuss American idioms.

It was not long before this student paused one day to ask, "Why do you do this for me? It seems to me you do not get paid to do this and that you are very decent people." In an instant, friendship opened the door to an evangelistic opportunity which ultimately led to this student's commitment to Christ. If students experience the love of Christ at first in you, they will ask you what makes you different.

For several months, Yang had been in a Northeastern Bible study. The study leader gave Yang some Christian literature and she read it alone. Later, Yang made a profession of faith to her friendship partner. She said, "I have been searching for God for a long time."

Care for the Student's Family

Estimates put the number of Chinese students in America at over 40,000, but this does not take into account a greater number of Chinese here who are spouses and families of these students. More than 60 percent of the Chinese students in the U.S. have brought along their spouses and families. In most cases, these spouses are women. Here are some facts about these student spouses:

- Most are college graduates.
- Many worked in China as teachers, engineers, technicians, and in many of the science fields.
- Most have been unable to continue their education in America be-

cause of financial difficulties. But some are part- or full-time students themselves.

- Even more than the students, these spouses tend to experience loneliness and isolation while here in the United States. This may be because of poor language skills, lack of transportation, caring for children, and the inability to obtain meaningful employment.

Christians working with Chinese students should seriously consider ministry among these spouses and families. In fact, these spouses are often more responsive to the Gospel, will be more active in Bible study and other activities, and may become the best Christian witness to their husbands or wives.

Zhou and Jing were students at George Washington University in Washington, D.C. During her time in the U.S., Jing became a Christian and attended church and Bible study on a regular basis. Though she gently tried to witness to her husband, Zhou showed no interest in Christianity. However, he would drive his wife every Sunday to church so that she could attend services because it was so important to her. While Jing attended church, Zhou would sit in the car and read the newspaper or study. Noticing this, the pastor of the church wisely approached Zhou while he was reading in the car and said, "You know, I have a very warm study in my office and I am not using it. Why don't you come in and use it each week while I am preaching and Jing is attending the service and Sunday school?"

The genuine and sincere offer touched Zhou's heart. Over the next few weeks, a friendship formed between the pastor and Zhou. Ultimately, Zhou felt free to discuss his beliefs and questions with his new friend. Over time, Zhou committed his life to Jesus Christ. He began attending Bible study with the pastor, who faithfully met with him through the year. One day, Zhou did not show up for Bible study. The pastor phoned his home only to find the number had been disconnected and that Zhou and Jing were gone. His fear and bewilderment were eliminated two weeks later when the phone in his study rang and he heard Zhou's voice: "I am sorry I did not call you, but I received a call from the government of my country to return home in twenty-four hours. I now have an important position in my government." Now Zhou leads a Bible study for a small group of friends each week.

Utilization of Chinese Student Believers

Approximately ten percent of the Chinese students in America are now Christians. Although a relatively small number, the potential impact of their witness should not be ignored. These Christian students come from two different backgrounds. Many received Jesus after arriving in the U.S. Less than one percent of the students came as Christians from China, were raised in Christian families, and/or were involved in China's house churches or the Three-Self church movement. These students tend to have strong and often dramatic testimonies of faith due to previous persecution, particularly during the Cultural Revolution.

These Chinese Christians are scattered across hundreds of college and university campuses in the country. Some are outgoing, expressive witnesses of Christ, eager to share the love of Christ with their fellow students. Other Chinese Christians will tend to be reserved and cautious about publicizing their faith.

JAPANESE

Japan sends more students to the United States than any other country except for the People's Republic of China. The vast majority of international students from Japan come here as non-Christians. These are Japan's best and brightest students, and a few follow some form of their country's traditional religions. For many others the rampant materialism and emerging individualism in Japanese society have squeezed out concern for spiritual matters.

Yet our window of opportunity to share Christ with these students is only for a few short years. Once the students graduate, they return home—where only one percent of the Japanese people are Christians.

A Natural Desire for Friendship

Most Japanese people desire friendship with people from other nations. As an island nation, Japan has been learning foreign ways and borrowing what it thought helpful for centuries. For the most part, Japanese have a natural curiosity about other parts of the world and are eager to learn from other cultures. This curiosity is true even more so for those Japanese who have ventured to other countries as international students, visiting scholars, or business people on assignment.

This desire for friendship, however, is not expressed in the same way it would be in Western culture. For some Japanese living overseas, showing initiative toward friendship is difficult and would be considered presumptuous. The Japanese person, when first overseas, feels like an outsider. You must, therefore, be ready for a lot of unilateral social outreach. Social politeness often dictates two or three refusals before an offer is accepted. Don't give up too soon.

Practical Tips for Developing Friendships

- In arranging a social contact with a Japanese person or family, make sure to *plan something* in particular and let your friend know the agenda when making the invitation. In Japan, social contacts are usually highly structured, especially at the outset.
- Take trips with Japanese people. They have a genuine fascination with the world and they love to travel. Day trips to local areas of interest are often a good way to befriend the Japanese.
- Arrange for a picture-viewing session. Whether slides, photographs, or videos, chances are that your friend has some visual record of the places he or she has visited.
- If your Japanese friend has an interest in sports, an introduction to the local sports facilities and a friendly match of tennis or round of golf would be much appreciated. With regard to spectator sports, taking in a professional baseball game makes a great outing, because baseball is extremely popular in Japan.
- Japanese women often enjoy cultural activities unique to the United States. Anything related to handmade crafts (e.g., quilt-making) is a particular favorite. Learning to prepare American foods is also appreciated.
- On the whole, Japanese are more interested in various forms of music than Americans. If there are concerts or musical programs offered in your area, invite an interested Japanese friend to attend with you.
- The Japanese also seem to be more interested in flowers and plants than Americans. A trip to a local plant conservatory or botanical garden will be enjoyed by most Japanese.

Social Reciprocity and Gift-Giving

The Japanese are gift-exchanging people. Early on in the friendship—often the first time they enter your home—they will bring a gift. You should express genuine thanks at the time you receive it and again when they are leaving the home. If you are invited to a Japanese home, make sure you bring a gift, however small, with you. In Japanese society, a gift given is to be met with a gift in return.

Gifts exchanged in Japan are similar to housewarming gifts in Western culture. Think of gifts that have great personal value rather than monetary value. One extremely valuable gift would be to introduce your friend to someone you know who is studying the same academic discipline or is involved in the same line of business as your friend. Because the Japanese are typically hesitant to introduce themselves to people on their own and usually rely on go-betweens for making new relationships, these types of introductions are highly appreciated.

Japanese Commitments to Family

Family ties in Japan are stronger than those in the West. Therefore, beginning a friendship with a Japanese means that you are beginning a friendship with that person's family. If family members visit, make sure that you show as much hospitality as possible. It's also a good idea to send a Christmas card and then a New Year's card to your Japanese friend's family back in Japan. Learn all you can about your friend's family and pray regularly for family members.

Some Japanese experience pressure from their families not to become too involved with Christianity, especially firstborn sons, who have the responsibility of continuing the worship of ancestors. A friendship that has included conversations on spiritual topics may go through a time of apathy on the part of your friend toward spiritual matters. Be patient. It is important that you respect your friend's spiritual comfort zone. If he or she is wary of Christians, be a genuine friend and pray for the right opportunity.

Horizontal Versus Vertical Friendships

Japanese society is vertically stratified. This means that one defines his identity by the people above or below him in social status. Status may be determined by age, wealth, education, occupation, and family. In fact, the society is so stratified that it even affects how a person speaks Japanese. Japanese speakers constantly monitor their audience and change the pronominal forms and verbal endings, depending on whether one is speaking *up* to someone of higher status or *down* to someone of lower status. Relationships among Japanese are thus vertically oriented, and can be called "vertical" friendships.

When a Japanese person goes overseas to countries with different social patterns, however, he or she is likely to anticipate some "horizontal" friendships, in which neither partner is concerned about status. Here are some practical steps toward developing a horizontal friendship with your Japanese acquaintance.

- Learn how to pronounce your friend's name. For the first several times you are together, ask for a brief check on pronunciation and for tips on how to say it better.
- Treat your friend with respect. If he or she has a Ph.D. or is an M.D., call him or her "Dr. ———" until your friend asks you to go on a first-name basis. If your friend wants to be called by a nickname, do so, but don't make up your own nickname for the person.
- Invite your friend into your home, including both of your families, if possible. Japanese couples and families who are overseas seem to enjoy experiencing things together.
- Be sensitive about what food you serve. It is usually best to serve a Western dish, as opposed to something that fits your stereotype of Japanese food.

Japanese Attitudes Toward Americans

Typically, Japanese people go through a "honeymoon period" at the outset of their stay in the States. During this time, they will focus on the positive aspects of American life: the open spaces, the variety and low cost of food, the friendly people, and the convenience of living in the United States. When you hear remarks along these lines, do not agree too quickly. Always respond that Japan has good points not always found in the Western world.

The "honeymoon period" will be followed by a time of increasing disillusionment with Western culture. Listen to your friend's criticisms of life here without interrupting and without defending your country. Then agree with the criticisms of American superficiality, selfish individualism, consumer waste, and the impersonal nature of American society. Any defense of your own country, even if motivated only by a desire to help your friend enjoy his or her stay, will merely reinforce the negative attitudes already in your friend's mind.

Gradually your Japanese friend will gain a more balanced perspective and be able to see both good and bad points to American society. This is the time when friendship can develop in a most genuine way.

During a going-away reception, three Japanese students approached an ISI staff member expressing their appreciation for their relationship with ISI. One student said, "You know, when we first came to the United States, the university matched us with some American families from the community. Later, you matched us with people from the church. We want you to know we saw a very big difference in the Christian people and the relationship they had with us. There is something very different about these people from the church, and we really appreciated our time with them."

The Religions of Contemporary Japan

Japanese who follow traditional religions do so for cultural reasons as opposed to deeply held spiritual beliefs.

Shinto

This religion is indigenous to Japan and is an essentially animistic religion that worships gods and goddesses in various aspects of nature. The religious rites that the world viewed during the accession of the emperor in 1989 are Shinto, for the emperor cult is a part of the Shinto religion.

The Japanese are religious pluralists, or engage in more than one religion. Christianity's slow growth within Japan this century has not simply been because Japanese will not accept Christianity, but because they will not accept it exclusively. If one were to present Christianity as simply another "insurance policy" along with Shinto and Buddhism, it would meet with a ready response. As you share the Gospel with your Japanese friend, make clear the exclusive claims of Jesus Christ (John 14:6) and those who followed Him (Acts 4:12). One way to emphasize the exclusive claims of Christ is to start with monotheism. This is a strange concept to the Japanese, since there are eight million gods and goddesses in Shinto. The best way to approach this concept is to explain the attributes of the one true God according to the Bible. Encourage your Japanese friend to read such texts as Exodus 10:3-6 and 34:6-7.

Buddhism

This religion entered Japan during the sixth century A.D. The roots of Buddhism in Japan are rather deep and to this day the religion is an integral part of the national identity.

There are several effective bridges between Buddhism and Christianity. From a historical perspective, you might ask your friend to review the teachings of the tenth-century Buddhist priest Kobo Daishi. This priest returned from studying in China with a form of Buddhism that contained a heaven, hell, and salvation through the merit of another. It can be documented that there were Nestorian Christians in the Chinese city where he studied. The influence from Christianity on Kobo Daishi's form of Buddhism makes it a helpful starting point for dialogue.

Westerners should understand that there are many varieties of Buddhism, just as there are various Christian denominations. If your friend is interested in Buddhism, you should listen carefully to the description he or she gives. Always try to understand before offering any answer or alternative to your friend's beliefs. Resist the urge to dispute a point before understanding (Proverbs 18:13).

Ancestor Worship

While not a religion itself, ancestor worship is a popular religious activity that is related to some forms of Buddhism. Ancestor worship may not seem to be a problem when sharing your faith in Christ with your Japanese friend. Your friend, however, may face extreme pressure to continue the tradition of worshiping at the family godshelf when he or she returns to Japan.

Two present-day examples show how vital this issue of ancestor worship is to Japanese considering Christianity. One Japanese man trusted in Christ and made a clean break with ancestor worship. A firstborn son, he asked his father to transfer his rights to the inheritance to his brother, since he would not continue the family's worship of ancestors. In God's time, this man's father and brother also became Christians, and the man and his brother are now pastors in Japan.

On the other hand, a Japanese man who is friends with an American Christian has seemed, at times, very close to making a complete identification with Jesus. But he refuses to be baptized, because he senses that if he takes this step, he will have to renounce his duties as firstborn to worship at the family godshelf. The spiritual warfare is especially intense with some forms of Buddhism—and always with ancestor worship. Ask God to deliver your friend into His kingdom.

Being an Effective Christian Witness to Japanese Students

Three guiding principles should guide your friendship with Japanese students.

Show Appreciation for the Japanese Culture

Because Japan emphasizes racial and cultural uniformity, you can only imagine how displaced your Japanese friend feels in our country. It is crucial, therefore, to show interest in and appreciation for the Japanese culture during the first months of your friend's stay here. Daily, your friend may be painfully aware of how inadequate his or her English skills are and how little he or she knows about living in this country. Affirm your friend in his or her knowledge of business or the academic discipline studied or simply his or her Japanese heritage.

The Importance of Sensitivity

As you encourage your friend, keep in mind that he or she has a different set of values and a different sense of humor than you do. The distinctives of your values and sense of humor, while a source of pride to your American individualism, may irritate your Japanese friend. James' advice is best: "Everyone should be quick to listen, slow to speak and slow to become angry" (James 1:19).

Show sensitivity in your use of the English language and your humor. Speak at a reasonable speed—too slow may come across as condescending and thus offensive—and speak distinctly. Americans tend to speak louder than people from other countries. We also can mistakenly think that speaking louder will remove difficulties in communication. Speaking loudly may be interpreted as anger by your Japanese friend. Therefore, keep your volume down when speaking to a Japanese. Also, do not alter your pronunciation. To do so is analogous to using "baby talk" with an adult.

The Example of Servanthood

An excellent way to avoid misunderstandings is to *be a servant*. You and the Gospel will gain credibility as you show yourself to be a servant on behalf of your friend. You can do this in many practical ways.

It also means that you will deliver on what you promise. Consider the implications before you tell your friend such things as "Don't hesitate to call me if I can be of help." A Japanese student will often interpret a casual remark as a commitment.

Good relationships take time to build. Credibility is gained over a period of time, but with God's help and patience your relationship will become one that bears fruit.

Sharing Jesus With the Japanese Student

These four themes have a particular resonance with the Japanese student.

God as the True Father

Much of the trouble all of us have in our spiritual walk stems from our incomplete understanding of God. It follows, therefore, that when you start to share Jesus Christ with your friend, you will want to ask about his or her understanding of God. Then, talk about how the Bible presents God as the Creator-Father who has a claim on humanity.

Japan is clearly a patriarchal society; the Japanese know what it means to have a human father. Since the Bible describes God as Father, this is a point to emphasize. The Shinto gods or various conceptions of Buddha do not have the theme of fatherhood.

Sin as Self-Centeredness

You may also emphasize that sin is a self-centered departure from one's true Father. While most Japanese do not have a clear idea of sin, they do acknowledge that self-centeredness is wrong. The problem of sin and self-centeredness has profoundly affected Japanese thought because of the widespread Buddhist influence in Japan.

You can explain the Fall as a self-centered move away from the true Father who took delight in creating and providing for humanity. This Fall is lived out in our lives when we pursue self-centered ends instead of God.

Jesus—the Ultimate "Go-Between"

Once the sin problem has been explained, you can go on to talk about Jesus as the ultimate "go-between." Japanese society operates through mediators, sometimes called "go-betweens." The biblical concept of Jesus as mediator, therefore, makes perfect sense to the Japanese once the condition of human alienation from God has been accepted.

Mark 15:37-39 shows how through Jesus' death God removed an obstacle between humanity and himself. Even now, Jesus is our "go-between" in the sense of his priestly role. Hebrews 4:14-16 shows this well. The status of Jesus as "go-between" has significant implications for our response to God.

A Return to the True Father

Because humanity is in a condition of desertion from its true Father, and because Jesus is the "go-between," our response to God should be one of dependence on the work of Jesus in his death and resurrection to bring us to God. 1 Corinthians 15:3 states that Christ died for our sins. This means that he bore the punishment that believing sinners deserve (1 John 2:1-2). Our responsibility as runaway humans, therefore, is to place all our hope of reaching God in Jesus (Acts 16:31).

Since Jesus is God's only Son, our only access to God is through Jesus (John 1:18, Acts 4:12). While other religions contain aspects of truth about the human condition, only the Bible explains the way back to our true Father—faith in Jesus Christ. Only through placing our faith in God's provision for covering our sin can we live with God (John 6:29, 1 John 4:10).

REACHING THE AFRICAN STUDENT

African students in the United States represent a significant and influential segment of Africa's elite. They will be the opinion leaders and change agents who chart the future course of their developing nations. In today's rapidly changing world, the innovations these future leaders will initiate will have global effects politically, educationally, socially, and spiritually.[2]

African Concepts of Religion and Christianity

"Animism," "ancestral worship cults," "primal religions," and other terms used by Western-trained anthropologists do not fully describe the African concept of religion. From the African perspective, religion—in whatever form—bears the following marks:

- It deals with a creator god who is transcendent—he created and sustains all creation.
- Creation includes the elements—sun, moon, stars, water, air, land, human and spirit beings, plants and animals.
- Religious experts must skillfully probe the spiritual and human realms, epitomize religion in their lifestyle, and be psychologically knowledgeable and spiritually powerful. These experts must remain adept at their practice to retain their supplicants.
- The practical benefits of a religion are more important than a structured and carefully drawn out set of beliefs.
- Religion permeates every area of human existence.

Concepts of Christianity

Africans generally divide Christianity into two streams—Christianity before colonialization, and Christianity during and after colonization.

The Ethiopian Orthodox and Egyptian Coptic Christianity—influenced by such early church leaders as Tertullian, Ireneus, Augustine, Cyprian, and Apollos—are examples of pre-colonialization Christianity.

Christianity closely associated with colonialization—primarily in sub-Saharan Africa—exists in daughter churches planted by Western missionaries during the colonial era. Typical examples include the Anglican, Presbyterian, and Methodist churches.

A third stream has also recently emerged, consisting of independent churches as well as Christian professional and student movements. These are African counterparts of such organizations as the Full Gospel Businessmen's Fellowship, International, Campus Crusade for Christ, and the Navigators in the United States.

African Students in the United States

Who Are They; Where Are They From?

Among the most popular fields of study for African students are business and management, engineering, mathematics and computer science, and physical, life, and social sciences. More than half of the African students studying on American campuses are enrolled in undergraduate studies. Thirty-eight percent are involved in graduate study and post-graduate programs. Most undergraduate students are funded by family and friends. Graduate students tend to draw their financial support from their home government or university, the American university where they attend, or international organizations.

African Students and Christianity

African students may be categorized by their response to the Christian faith.

Christian students

Although African Christians are a minority of the African students coming to the United States, these students can play a vital role in local churches and international student ministry. There are two types of African Christian students: mature believers who may have played an active leadership role in local churches or ministries, and young or new believers who may have accepted Christ only a short while before coming to the United States or during their stay here.

Because of their ministry experience, the mature Christians can be highly effective in reaching out to other international students. They can also contribute significantly to the local churches they attend in America. What these students need most is additional training and the opportunity for lay-leadership roles in ministry.

Young or new Christians, on the other hand, may be highly susceptible to backsliding while in America. Therefore, these students have a critical need for follow-up, discipleship, and Bible study to build their faith.

Muslim students: Free from the governmental and cultural restraints they often face in their own countries, Muslim students in the United States are often more open to the Gospel during their studies here. With patience, tact, and sensitivity—getting to know these students and becoming involved in their lives—American Christians can help interest Muslim students in exploring the Good News of Jesus Christ.

Secularistic Students

Secularistic students relate easily to contemporary American society. They can also easily make American friends. If American Christians don't reach out to these students, especially in the critical first few weeks and months they are here, they may return to Africa even more closed to the

Gospel than they were before they arrived.

Many of these students have been exposed to and have already made up their minds about Christianity before coming to the United States. Many have attended church-oriented schools and colleges—and the mandatory worship services there. Some have been approached by insensitive Christian activists on university campuses in Africa. Others have bought into the prevailing unpopular image of clergy in African society. Consequently, many have forged negative views about Christianity.

Some of these negative views include the following:

- Christianity is anti-intellectual. Because most African pastors are not highly educated, Christianity is thought by many African students to be fit only for "dropouts," the aged, and the lowest classes of society.
- Christianity is only concerned with the human soul. The Christian God is often presented as a soul-saving, hero God who has no concern for the mind and body.
- Christianity contains inconsistencies. God is portrayed as powerful yesterday, but is thought to be no match for local evil spirits and witches today. Christianity advocates a loving God but is practiced by Christian groups who are often intolerant and unloving toward others.
- Christianity is a religion of impractical beliefs. While Christianity stresses the importance of adhering to its beliefs, the practice of these beliefs has not noticeably improved human relations and lifestyles in "Christian" societies. In fact, it often isolates and insulates its adherents from human needs.

For secularistic students, these negative views of Christianity are the basis of resentment and rejection. Such notions reinforce Marx's view of religion as "the opiate of the people." Many African elite have concluded: "Christianity is the handmaiden of Western colonization and the exploitation of Africa."

Secularistic students often come to the United States to explore and experience American democratic institutions and to see how they differ from other forms of government. They try to discern how the principles underlying these institutions and government can be adapted to nation-building in modern Africa. Of course, we know that true spiritual faith is vital for all institutions and governments.

Many of these students arrive determined to discover and walk in the footprints of their predecessors who, while they studied here in the 1940s, caught the spirit and love of self-rule and then returned home to liberate their countries from colonial rule. These students want to make a difference in their countries' governments and histories. It's urgent to befriend these students with the love of Jesus Christ. American Christians need to reach them early.

Hurdles to Effective Ministry

Stereotypes: Not only do Africans have misconceptions about the United States, Americans have misconceptions about Africa. Hollywood, as well as *National Geographic* (among other periodicals), stereotypically portray the "safari" image of Africa—picturing Africans as loyal servants of their "Tarzan" white masters. The image of Africa as a "dark" continent is further perpetuated by Western media coverage of famine and political unrest in African nations.

American Christians (no matter how well-meaning) who approach secularistic African students from such perspectives will not succeed in reaching these students with the Good News of Jesus Christ.

Christianity and Culture

When sharing the Gospel, you must take into account three cultures—your own, that of your African friend, and the cultural context of the Bible. Therefore, you should sensitively consider your African friend's cultural perspective and tailor your Gospel presentation accordingly. To do this, you must first seek to know and understand your friend and his or her culture.

As you open your honest hearts to students from other lands, let them know

1. that you love them for Christ's sake;

2. that you will be their friend;

3. that probably both you and the students will make culturally sensitive mistakes;

4. that the friendship is to be an enjoyable experience for everyone;

5. that openness and honesty will be vital tools of adequate communication together.

Apply What You Have Learned

1. Each section of this chapter contains practical principles to use in your evangelism efforts with Muslim students, Chinese students, Japanese students, or African students.
2. How can you become increasingly more effective with students from these areas of the world?
3. Order the country profile that corresponds to the student(s) you will be or are already ministering to. Also, obtain the people-group-specific booklet in ISI's *Sharing the Good News* booklet series to learn more about ministry to your particular student. See Appendix A.
4. Plan a strategy to utilize what you have learned in this chapter.

NINE

Studying the Bible With International Students

"For you have been born again, not of perishable seed, but of imperishable, through the living and enduring word of God."

1 Peter 1:23

Martiza Crespo from Venezuela was already a Christian when she arrived in Ann Arbor to begin her graduate studies. Before long, she joined an ISI staff member in regular Bible study. Later she returned to Caracas and told the staff member, "The Friday group meetings changed my life. I learned how to have a prayer meeting and a Bible study group. I am teaching a discipleship class in one of the toughest 'barrios' in Caracas. Last Wednesday I had thirteen people and we keep on growing." Martiza also travels to other South American countries and trains women to lead Bible studies.

To study the Bible with another person, you don't need a seminary degree. Bible study can be nothing more than two friends discussing biblical truths together. All you need are the right resources, prayer support, and perhaps a little guidance. A one-to-one Bible study provides a relaxed, unhurried atmosphere in which your friend can examine biblical truths, raise spiritual doubts, and perhaps struggle through the process of making a decision for Christ.

Your role in leading a Bible study is to guide your international friend through the discovery process in the Christian faith. Your friend may be anywhere along the continuum of this discovery process—from no knowledge of Jesus Christ to a total acceptance of the Savior. Wherever your friend stands, you must be totally accepting of where he or she is and not make spiritual progress a condition of your relationship.

As your friend observes your life or informally discusses spiritual issues with you, he or she may want to learn more about your faith in Christ. This may lead him or her to become interested in studying the Bible with you.

Is Your Friend Ready to Study the Bible?

Before you begin a Bible study with your international friend, take a moment to evaluate whether or not your friend is ready to receive the Gospel. Check each of these points and decide whether you agree with the statement or not. If you do, make a check mark by the statement.

Is a relationship under way?

☐ We have spent time together.
☐ We have exchanged basic information about each other.
☐ We have made formal or informal plans to see each other again.

Is there freedom in the relationship?

☐ We like each other.
☐ We feel comfortable around each other.
☐ We each take initiative in spending time together and appreciate that time.
☐ There is fun and laughter when we are together.

Is there trust in the relationship?

☐ We share and keep information confidential.
☐ We speak well of each other to other people.
☐ We ask each other for favors.
☐ We have an active awareness of each other's needs.
☐ We entrust responsibility to each other.

Is there acceptance in the relationship?

☐ We are not threatened by our differences (religion, culture, personality, habits, tastes, and values) and are able to discuss these differences.

☐ We are open to learning from each other.

☐ We are sincere in our conversation—we listen attentively and remember shared information.

☐ We are frank—we say what we feel without fear of threatening our relationship.

Does your friend understand the concept of being a "Christian?"

☐ My friend identifies me as a serious, rather than cultural, Christian.

☐ I have shared my personal testimony, both about my conversion and what Christ means to me.

☐ My friend has heard or read other testimonies that have reinforced mine.

☐ My friend knows other committed Christians.

Is your friend interested in Christianity?

☐ My friend asks me questions about my faith.

☐ My friend has attended a church service or other Christian activity.

☐ My friend has expressed a desire to meet Christians.

☐ My friend has expressed an interest in reading and discussing the Bible.

If you checked most of the applicable boxes above (probably no one will be able to check all of them and not every question may apply to your relationship), then your international friend is prepared to begin studying the Bible. If not, you may want to let your relationship develop further before attempting to study the Bible together.

BEFORE YOU BEGIN

Bible Study Materials

International Students, Incorporated has developed several Bible studies (see Appendix B) designed especially for use with international students. These Bible studies require little or no preparation on the part of the international student. The Bible passages are often written in an easy-to-read translation in the study guides themselves, making it easy for students to make notes in the margins and define words they do not understand.

These studies emphasize discovering the Word of God through personal investigation. One study is called *I AM* and leads the student through the various claims of Jesus Christ, while the second study, titled *Jesus the Liberator*, examines the teachings of Jesus Christ. These studies are designed to help the international student consider and understand the claims of Jesus Christ and make personal decisions based on what they learn. Each Bible study contains a leader's guide which can help you answer questions your friend may raise.

Make Sure Your Friend Has a Bible

Although the ISI Bible studies often have the passages written in the study guides, your international friend should have his or her own Bible for personal reading and study. You may want to give your friend a Bible as a gift; however, some people tend to place more value on something they buy themselves.

Help your friend find a Bible in a readable translation, such as the *New International Version*, the *New Living Translation* or the *Contemporary English Version*. (The CEV is designed for a third grade reading level.) The version you select should correspond with the version you will use during the Bible study. For example, if you have a *New International Version*, help your international friend find the same. Then you will both be reading from the same text when you read and study together.

An English Bible is helpful for your study together, but a Bible in your friend's native language is important for his or her complete understanding of the passages. Encourage your friend to look up the passages in both English and his or her native language before your meeting. Elsewhere in Appendix A we share how to secure various language Bibles.

Your international friend may prefer to study the Bible in English in order to improve his or her proficiency. If so, encourage your friend to read the passage beforehand, looking up any words he or she does not understand. Understanding the passage is the most important aspect of the reading process.

When to Meet

Remember, most international students are here for one primary purpose—to earn an academic degree. As a result, their time schedule will be busy and oftentimes hectic. Ask your international friend about his or her schedule, and find the most appropriate day of the week and time of the day for both of you to meet regularly. Maintain this regular schedule, but be flexible because exam times, term papers, and other special events may require special scheduling.

Your Bible study should last at least 50 minutes but no longer than an hour and a half. (This time will accommodate open periods between classes.) However, if your friend has the time and wants to talk further, your conversation may be extended longer than planned. These can be special meetings, so don't schedule yourself so tightly that you can't take advantage of them. At the same time, remember your friend's schedule and don't go too long past the planned meeting time.

If your international friend has difficulty making the study on time, it doesn't mean he or she doesn't care. As we have emphasized already, some cultures place a different value on time. Or perhaps your friend couldn't get in touch with you. Whatever the case, be flexible and understanding.

Where to Meet

If your schedule allows, meet your international friend on campus. This shows you are willing to accommodate your friend rather than expecting to be accommodated. However, you will need to be sensitive to your friend's religious and cultural background. For example, a Muslim will often receive great pressure from fellow Muslims if they discover he or she is studying the Bible with you. For this reason, your home or other location away from campus may be the best choice.

If meeting on campus is not a problem, look for a place that is quiet, appropriately lighted, out of the way, and available. Places such as the library, cafeteria, or a dorm room can provide the right atmosphere for study.

Don't forget to begin with prayer. Before you start meeting with your international friend (and throughout the Bible study), pray for God's guidance, for his revelation to your friend through the study, and for the penetration of the Holy Spirit through God's Word into your friend's life. Most importantly, pray for your friend no matter what his or her response to the Gospel message might be. And don't try to go it alone. Get others to pray for your Bible study and for your international friend.

Later in the study, when you sense your friend feels comfortable, you may want him or her to begin and/or end each study with a time of prayer. However, be sensitive to your friend's needs and expectations (for example, don't require your friend to bow his head, but simply allow him to listen as you pray).

Be Sensitive

Here are a couple of issues to consider before starting your Bible study:

- The teacher should be as old or older than the student. Most cultures place a high degree of respect on age. Your friend may not attribute much credibility to you as a teacher if you are younger.
- The teacher and student should be of the same gender, unless there is an obvious age difference. A male teacher should never meet with a female student alone. He should bring along a Christian woman (who could learn to lead a similar study with another female student, if she does not already know how to lead one).

INSIDE THE WORD

When your international friend has agreed on a place and what to study, you are ready to begin.

Stick to the Bible

When you begin the Bible study, your friend may not believe the Bible is the Word of God. Accept that possibility. Both of you must understand that the purpose is to find out what the Bible teaches about Jesus, and not to debate personal opinions. Discussion about the reliability of biblical accounts should be postponed until a later time or even a separate study. The Word of God is powerful, and its truths can penetrate and convict even the most skeptical person—in God's timing.

Some "Bible studies" may turn into philosophical discussions on peripheral issues such as, "How can a loving God judge people?" or "What happens to people from cultures that have never heard the Gospel?" Avoid tangents. If a particular question seems to be a real obstacle to your friend, ask if you can get back to him or her next week, and then take the time to research the issue.

Answer questions using the Bible as much as possible. For instance, if your friend asks, "Why are so many intelligent people atheists?" direct him or her to 1 Corinthians 1:27 and surrounding passages: "But God chose the foolish things of the world to shame the wise. . . ."

Above all, avoid arguments of any kind. You may win the argument, but you will not be displaying Christ's love. Your friend's belief system— though it may be incorrect in certain areas—is still very important to him or her. Making light of or condemning your friend's beliefs will only drive him or her further away from Jesus Christ. Discussions are appropriate; arguments are not. Concentrate on presenting the truths of Christianity through God's Word, and let the Holy Spirit do the convicting.

Start With the Basics

Western Christians have a tendency to start with the Book of Romans and then lay out the Gospel in a neat doctrinal system that is expected to persuade anyone to accept Christ. This approach fails to recognize that someone who adheres to a different religion may not have even a foundational understanding of the existence and role of God in the universe and his sovereign role in human life. As a result, you may need to start from "square one," presenting God's existence. How do we know there is a God? How can we know the Truth? Present God in his work of creation and his authority over mankind as outlined in Genesis 1–3. Use the ISI new video tool called *New Beginnings*, which covers the basics in fifteen-minute segments covering these topics: Salvation, Assurance, Lordship, the Bible, Prayer, the Holy Spirit, and Witnessing.

Using the video for fifteen minutes each week and accompanying that with a 30- to 45-minute study of the appropriate lesson in the accompanying workbook will assist you in easily discussing the basics of the Christian life (see Appendix B).

Also, many people from other cultures have never heard of Jesus. If your friend has not heard of Jesus or has little knowledge of who he is, you will need to present Jesus as a person—his character, his works, and his claims—as shown throughout the New Testament accounts. The ISI Bible study *I AM* is a good place to start because it effectively accomplishes this objective.

To present the Gospel in its entirety at the beginning of an evangelistic study would be like giving steak and potatoes to an infant. It would be completely indigestible. Instead, give your international friend milk, not solid food. Bring the individual along slowly, presenting Jesus Christ as a person and letting the Holy Spirit persuade your friend to seek a relationship with the Savior.

As you study portions of the Gospel accounts, opportunities will arise to explain the complete Gospel. At some point in your study, you should fully explain Christ's death and resurrection and how these events enable all people to enter into a right relationship with the Savior.

Make sure your friend knows how to accept Christ if he or she desires to do so. But don't force your friend or exert your own pressure (rather than the Holy Spirit's conviction) on him or her to make a premature decision. Most people hear the Gospel many times before responding to it. Your friend may need to hear numerous presentations of the Gospel before it becomes clear.

No Strings Attached

As you begin the study, your international friend may fear that your friendship is conditioned upon his or her response to Christ. Let your friend know that your friendship is a "no strings attached" relationship. If he or she does not want to start or continue the Bible study, it's not a reflection on you or the student.

Under no circumstances should you discontinue the friendship because of your friend's response (or lack of it) to the Gospel message or your invitation to study the Bible together.

As the study progresses, your friend may become more open, but may continue to struggle with doubts or the cost of following Christ. Encourage him to openly express his feelings. Try to provide a non-threatening atmosphere in which to discuss his questions. Make it clear that you accept him and his opinions, even if you do not necessarily agree. Remember, only God's spirit can give spiritual insight.

Avoid Jargon

Many Christian terms today are difficult even for churched Americans to understand. International students who come from different religious backgrounds and have difficulty with English will be confused if we use doctrinal terms without stopping to explain what they mean. Religious terms also may have a different meaning in other religions and cultures.

For example, the term "born again" may mean reincarnation to a Buddhist or Hindu.

Things to Remember

Here are some additional guidelines for effective Bible study:

- Show you care about your international friend's progress not only in the Bible study but also in the classroom. Ask questions about his or her studies, how classes are going, and how you may be of assistance.
- Write down things as you speak. This will not only help your international friend "see" what you are saying, but it provides a record of your study. (Make sure your friend is in a position to see what you are writing.)
- Contribute freely to the conversation, but don't do all the talking.
- Be enthusiastic and friendly.
- Wait until your friend has finished discussing a point before responding.
- Don't be defensive about your faith or what the Bible says. The Holy Spirit and the Word of God are powerful enough to defend themselves.
- Be gentle in responding to a statement or point of view. Don't argue.
- Stick to the topic, but be sensitive to your friend's need to simply "talk." More positive witnessing can often be accomplished in informal discussion than in theological discourse.
- Avoid stifling the interaction with "cut-and-dried" answers. If your friend feels that you are not open to truly hearing ideas because you already have "the answer," he or she will not respond as openly and interaction will deteriorate.
- When stating answers, preface them with the phrase: "This is what the Bible says." Your answers should come authoritatively from God, not personal opinion.
- Be flexible. Don't feel that you need to complete one lesson each week. Your friend may need more time to discuss particular issues. Rather than trying to rush through a lesson at one sitting, extend the discussion as needed.
- Once again, the goal of the Bible study is to increase spiritual awareness, not necessarily to convert your friend to your faith or thinking.

ASKING QUESTIONS

Christ often used questions to provoke thought or bring forth affirmation of belief. A truth will be more meaningful to your friend if he or she personally discovers it through guided discussion rather than simply having it "preached." *A truth understood is more meaningful than a truth recited.*

The questions in the ISI Bible study guides have been designed for the purpose of getting students to read and think about the text on their own by testing their comprehension of its teaching through a series of questions. As the discussion takes place, however, don't hesitate to add your own questions to stimulate thought. In the ISI Bible studies, there are three primary types of questions: observation, interpretation, and application.

Observation Questions

Observation questions ask, "How do the truths of this passage affect my life?" and begin with words such as *who, what, when, where, find, list,* and *describe.* Getting the facts straight is essential before interpretation of the passage can begin.

Observation questions also give you a chance to quickly test your friend's comprehension of the passage. You may be surprised at how much insight your friend has. However, he or she will probably need occasional help to understand the passage's cultural context.

Interpretation Questions

Interpretation questions ask, "What does the passage mean?" and begin with words such as *why, how,* and *explain.* Ask yourself which words and phrases may not be clearly understood and develop clarifying questions such as, "What do you think this word means?" These questions should be related to the truth discovered through the observation questions.

Application Questions

Application questions ask, "What does the passage mean to me here and now?" Simply knowing truth makes no difference in a person's life unless it is applied in some way (James 1:22-25). Ask how people in your friend's culture would react to the passage and why.

In addition, ask questions such as, "How could knowing this truth about God make a difference in your life?" Since your friend is still probably investigating Christianity, be careful not to ask questions that are too direct or personal, or questions that pressure your friend to make a premature decision. For example, instead of asking, "Are you a Christian?" ask, "How does one become a Christian?"

Note: You may need to postpone application questions until you get deeper into the study (a period of weeks) so as not to confuse your friend. Make sure you lay the foundation of the Gospel before moving to application questions.

Practical Guidelines

Here are some additional points to remember as you develop questions:

- Make sure your questions are well understood. Use clear, concise language without idioms or difficult words. Rephrase the question if your friend does not understand you. You may want to write out the question on paper for better understanding.
- Try to avoid yes or no questions. Inquiries such as "Did Jesus die on the cross to save us?" leave little room for discussion. Instead, ask, "Why did Jesus die on the cross?" (Sometimes you'll need to ask yes or no questions as a first step, but follow with "why" or "explain" questions.)
- Never assume an answer. Your friend will feel pressured into answering a certain way if you ask a question such as, "Jesus died on the cross to save us, didn't he?"
- Ask opinion questions ("What's your opinion. . . ?") to see if your friend is understanding the material.
- Ask "feeling" questions in addition to "fact" questions. "Feeling" questions deal with your friend's reaction to the discovered truth. "What do you think about that?" or "How does that make you feel?"
- Be prepared to wait for an answer. Don't be afraid of silence. Your friend may need time to think about his or her answer, or may need time to formulate the answer in English. Rephrase your question if necessary, or guide your friend to the right place in the text, but don't be hasty to give the answer yourself.
- Listen attentively. Show your friend that you are interested through

facial expressions, eye contact, and by responding sincerely to what has been said. If you do not understand your friend's answer, rephrase what you think he or she said and ask if that is what was meant. If you sense that your friend has more to say, ask, "Would you like to add anything to that?" Ask further questions based on the responses given.

- Give praise for involvement ("good answer"). To help your friend "save face" when correcting an answer, make statements such as "Good answer. How about looking at it this way?" or "Good answer. Here's what the Bible says. . . ."

Stop and Evaluate Along the Way

After several lessons together, you will want to evaluate your friend's progress. The following checklist will help:

Has the Bible been discussed?

☐ My friend owns a Bible in his or her own language (preferably) as well as English.

☐ We have discussed the characteristics of the Bible—its origin, its authorship (God's Word), and its reliability.

☐ My friend shows an interest in the Bible studies.

☐ A "healthy" tension exists in my friend's life as he or she deals with God's truth.

Does your friend have a sufficiently accurate picture of Jesus Christ?

☐ My friend has a biographical knowledge of Jesus Christ.

☐ My friend understands Jesus' claims of deity.

☐ My friend's information is based on the Bible rather than hearsay.

Has the Gospel message been explained?

☐ My friend knows, after several lessons, the irreducible core of the Gospel that one must believe to become a Christian.

☐ My friend has verbalized a clear understanding of the Gospel.

☐ My friend senses a need to respond to the message of Christ.

☐ My friend knows how to receive Christ.

Has a personal decision been faced?

☐ My friend is clearly aware that the next step is his or hers to take.
☐ My friend knows that a personal decision is required.
☐ My friend has been asked to make a commitment.
☐ My friend has considered the personal costs involved in following Christ.
☐ My friend knows that I will remain a friend no matter what he or she decides.

Making the Decision

If your friend makes a decision to follow Christ, ask yourself the following questions:

☐ Was the commitment made privately or with someone else?
☐ Has my friend verbalized the decision to me?
☐ Has my friend received help with the assurance of salvation?
☐ Is my friend being discipled or trained in the basics of the Christian walk?

Here is a special word of caution if your friend is from a country that is hostile to Christians or Christianity.

- Be very discreet when talking to others about your international friend.
- If your friend makes a decision for Christ, let him or her determine when, where, or if it should be made public—he or she could face severe persecution if certain people know.

Studying the Bible with your international friend is perhaps the greatest simple approach to guide him to the truth. Truth sets a person free. Faith in God's truth in Christ secures personal salvation when received by an individual through confession, repentance from sin, and faith in Christ. Bible study together can be an adventure, a discovery for the international student and for the friendship partner.

"Faith comes from hearing the message, and the message is heard through the word of Christ" (Romans 10:17).

Apply What You Have Learned

1. Think for a moment about the value of God's Word in your own life. How can you share this testimony with an international student?

2. Select the best evangelistic or basic Bible study to help you in your early discussions with your international friend.
3. Share how to have a twenty-minute daily quiet time:
   Five minutes—talking to God (prayer).
   Ten minutes—listening to God (reading his Word).
   Five minutes—applying God's truth to your life today.
4. Be available to join your student in a deeper Bible study (even if you meet only once every four to six weeks). Or, make sure your student is in a study if you are not available.

TEN

The Shock of Reentry

"I will go before you and will level the mountains; I will break down gates of bronze and cut through bars of iron."

Isaiah 45:2

"But you will receive power when the Holy Spirit comes on you; and you will be my witnesses in Jerusalem, and in all Judea and Samaria, and to the ends of the earth."

Acts 1:8

A Filipino student came to the United States and studied. Shortly after returning home, he sent a letter to his American friendship partner about coming back to his home country. He wrote, "We are spiritually convinced that God put us here, but our American bodies and minds would rather be in Bloomingdale's or Macy's. Socially we feel upper middle class but physically we feel like below the poverty line. It's like living in a California condo in the middle of Harlem. For breakfast, I eat my favorite—pancakes topped with bananas and imitation maple syrup, while listening to *The Voice of America* with my American wife. It is a daily reminder that we have materially moved from the penthouse to the bottom floor. After my devotions, I go to the post office to get our mail. On the way, I have to walk through mud. I ask for some stamps. She tells me they do not have any stamps, but I'm fortunate because the stamp machine is working. It's like going to an ice cream parlor that does not serve any ice cream. Then I step on a dilapidated bus that will pass through dilapidated roads.

"Before we left the United States, our friends envied us because we will live like kings here. I don't know of any king who has to walk through mud to get his mail. Actually, the physical part is the easiest part of our adjustment. What is much harder is the cultural, political, and emotional part of the adjustment. It is much harder than when I first came to the U.S. When I return to my own country, I feel like a foreigner."

This experience is mirrored in the lives of many international students when they return home.

The Shock Ahead—In Reverse

While the student may or may not be aware of it consciously, his period of time in the United States has changed him. He has grown as an individual in academics, in adaptability to a new place, and in making new friendships.

Because he has changed, he will experience a unique shock upon returning home. It's called reverse culture shock. Many students are not aware of this and don't prepare for it. You can help your international friend by talking to him about this very real possibility. Dr. Gary Weaver says, "When we anticipate a stressful event, we cope with it much better. We rehearse our reactions, think through the course of adjustment, and consider alternative ways to deal with the stressful event. . . . The most effective way to minimize the severity and duration of reverse culture shock is to anticipate its occurrence."[1]

When the student anticipates the process of readjustment, it is no guarantee that he or she will bypass all uncomfortable moments upon return. For example, some returnees inadvertently try to recreate their lifestyle in the United States. Others attempt to suppress or deny the influences of their U.S. educational experience and seek to return to their former life patterns. Some try to change their home environment, get frustrated, and either leave or associate with other people who have gone abroad and feel the same way they feel. This "flight" behavior during readjustment is often accompanied by a sense of disorientation—not being able to "connect" with peers. One may dream about returning to America for additional studies, or feel trapped in what is perceived as a hopeless situation.

For those students who delay returning home for years, the struggle to fit in at home is particularly difficult. These students have become totally absorbed with life in America. Only occasionally have they written back home to friends and family. Research indicates that these students will probably experience greater reentry-related problems on their return because the changes in themselves and at home will catch them by surprise. If a student is expecting an extended time away from his homeland, it is money well spent to return home every one or two years for a visit.

These are just a few of the practical pitfalls of reentry for internationals. No one can fully eliminate the low periods of emotional adjustment when entering a new culture or returning home. Returning students should expect varying degrees of stress and ineffectiveness during these times. But proper preparation can actually reduce the adjustment period. Preparation is the best prescription, and helping your international friend know that pitfalls exist can keep him or her from stepping in a hole.

Give Your International Friend a Head Start

Reverse culture shock can be overcome through some simple steps, such as maintaining regular contact with friends and family by phone and letters. Also, the establishment of regular routines, such as work, diet, and exercise, helps the student foster a sense of regularity, whether he is in another country or at home.

Years ago, Lisa Espineli-Chinn was an international student in the United States. She writes about her own reentry to her country in the introduction to a book called *Think Home*, saying, "My own reentry preparation, after three years of graduate study and service in the U.S., was a day set aside to review, reflect, check my attitudes, look to the Word and pray for God's strength to return home as his servant. Although that special day helped me in many ways, I wish I had had the benefit of broader reentry material." From this personal need, Espineli-Chinn created the workbook called *Think Home*.

At some point early in your relationship with the international student, you should give him or her a copy of *Think Home*. The workbook provides blank spaces for the student to record some significant highlights of his or her time in the United States. The guide also helps the student focus attention toward home, changes undergone, expectations from people there, and opportunities at home for ministry and service.

While *Think Home* covers the aspect of reentry thoroughly, some of the material is useful for friendship partners in understanding internationals. We've excerpted pertinent portions of the booklet in the following pages.

The Reentry Process

When a student returns home, they will feel at home and a foreigner at the same time. The international's feelings will swing from excitement to exhaustion, enjoyment to frustration. This emotional turbulence and tension is a very normal part of the transition process. "Continuing reentry stress," says Dr. Clyde Austin, a Christian psychologist and editor of two reentry books, "is normal for six to twelve months. A significant minority may experience readjustment stress beyond that point."[2]

People in transition often go through these stages: *Fun* is where everything is working fine. They are full of anticipation and excitement about returning home and are often received back with celebrity status because of their studies abroad. *Flight* is when the international's time as a celebrity is over, and he or she is faced with the daily demands of work and life back home. The person begins to wish for life back in the United States. *Fight* is the next stage, when the person has a lot of frustration and anger toward their home situation and begins to criticize and distance themselves from other people. *Fit* happens when the person is able to resolve their inner conflicts, find a place back home, and feel confident that they are making a positive contribution to others. As the student understands these stages of transition, it helps him understand himself better and thus enables him to handle the adjustment in a mature manner.

Returning home is like being in two worlds. Dr. Miriam Adney, a Christian anthropologist, tells her students that they "will never be able to go home again . . . they will probably always leave part of themselves behind, and thereafter be split . . . and home may be more than one place. But that is the price they pay for the richness of having experienced more than one culture deeply."[3]

Taking Inventory of Changes

You can help the international student understand the changes that have occurred in him through a personal inventory that is included as a

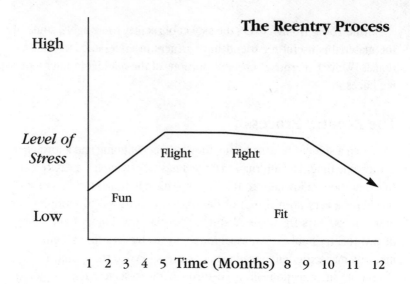

The Reentry Process

High

Level of Stress

Flight   Fight

Fun

Low   Fit

1   2   3   4   5 Time (Months) 8   9   10   11   12

part of *Think Home*. Here are some of the questions:
How Much Have You Changed?

Physically
1. Have you gained or lost weight?
2. Do you prefer American food?
3. Are you more (or less) conscious of your physical appearance or "image"?
4. How has your choice of clothes changed?

Socially
1. Are you more (or less) outgoing or shy?
2. How has your attitude toward the opposite sex changed?
3. Have you changed your manner or attitude toward older people?
4. Are you more (or less) class/status conscious?
5. Do you prefer being or living by yourself?

Academically
1. Do you feel more (or less) academically competent?
2. How has your relationship with your professors changed?
3. What study habits have you changed or maintained?

Emotionally

1. Are you more (or less) free to express your feelings to others?
2. Are you handling your emotions (happiness, anger, disappointment) differently now than you did at home?

Politically

1. How much attention have you paid to the political situation?
2. To what degree have your attitudes about politics been affected by the U.S. media, professors, fellow students, or other people?
3. Have your views concerning the role of government back home, or concerning U.S. foreign policy changed?

Financially

1. In what ways have you changed your opinion and/or handling of money and material wealth? Have your buying habits or "tastes" changed?
2. Are you more (or less) generous with your money or possessions?

Spiritually

1. How has your attitude changed regarding the religious beliefs and practices of your family and/or friends back home?
2. To what degree have your theological or doctrinal views changed?
3. Is your relationship with God stronger/weaker?

With regard to purpose and ambition?

1. How has your purpose or goals in life changed?
2. Would you consider your foreign experience life-changing? Why?

Developing a Spiritual Support Group

If your international friend has become a Christian or would like to have an ongoing relationship with Christians in his or her homeland, you can help him or her develop a spiritual support group. God's family is worldwide. ISI has a Global Follow-up Network worldwide to provide a mature Christian friend or mentor for each returning Christian student who is interested in having one. Contact ISI for further information or help.

As a student anticipates returning home, he should consider how he would feel about having friends in the U.S. committed to pray for and encourage him after he returns home. If he wants this type of prayer support, encourage him to list friends who would be willing to pray for him, then begin enlisting their pledge of prayer support.

As a friendship partner, you can help the international student locate fellowship and support in their home country. Our address:

International Students, Incorporated
Global Follow-Up Network
P.O. Box C
Colorado Springs, CO 80901

Potential Reentry Problems

Every international will experience some adjustments when he or she returns home. The degree of difficulty will vary, depending on each person's maturity, unique situation, and reentry preparation. The following list is a compilation of some of the problems returnees experience. You can help your international friend by giving him a copy of this checklist or possibly using it as a springboard for conversation before he or she returns home.

Cultural Adjustment

- [ ] Identity confusion—who are you now?
- [ ] Unrealistic expectations
- [ ] Changes in lifestyle
- [ ] Changes in fashion
- [ ] Localized or "provincial" mentality of relatives and friends
- [ ] Different concept of time
- [ ] Different pace of life (faster or slower)
- [ ] Family or community pressure to conform

Social Adjustment

- [ ] Loneliness and alienation
- [ ] Envy and distrust in interpersonal relations
- [ ] Tension between individual- and family-centeredness
- [ ] Feelings of superiority due to international experience and travel
- [ ] New and different interests from local peers
- [ ] Lack of modern conveniences
- [ ] Role or status changes
- [ ] Dissatisfaction with some ritualized patterns of social interaction

☐ Indifference of friends and relatives to your foreign experience; lack of serious, interested, and willing listeners to your stories

☐ Adjustment to noise, pollution, crowds, city congestion, unsanitary conditions, etc.

Communication Barriers

☐ Adoption of verbal and nonverbal codes that are not familiar to your countrymen

☐ Speech mannerisms that may be misinterpreted

☐ Impatience with roundabout, indirect communication styles

☐ Absence of colleagues who speak the same "language"

☐ Unfamiliarity with new forms of communication and styles of expression; current jargon and slang

National and Political Problems

☐ Changes in country's conditions, national priorities, policies, views

☐ Political climate not helpful to professional activity and/or advancement

☐ Economic uncertainties and conditions

☐ Changes in leadership, ruling parties

☐ Bureaucracy—how efficient and effective?

☐ Reluctance to live in a setting of political uncertainty

☐ Dissatisfaction with political situation

☐ Observed lack of national goals

Educational Problems

☐ Relevance of U.S. education to home situation

☐ Lack of facilities and resources for research or application of skills

☐ Absence of professional education programs to keep up with new developments and knowledge in the field

☐ Little opportunity to improve skills

☐ Incomplete fulfillment of educational goals in the U.S. and its implications back home

Professional Problems

☐ Inability to work in chosen specialty

☐ Facing oversupply in the job market/no openings

- [ ] Absence or inadequate translation of foreign scientific terminology
- [ ] Feeling of superiority due to U.S. training
- [ ] Isolation from academic or scientific developments in the U.S. and in own field
- [ ] Nonrecognition or appreciation of foreign degree
- [ ] Jealousy of colleagues
- [ ] Unrealistic expectations (job position, salary, what a U.S. degree "should" bring, etc.)
- [ ] Low compensation; few benefits
- [ ] Concern with quick material success; impatience with rate of promotion
- [ ] Perceived lack of enthusiasm and/or commitment among co-workers

Spiritual Problems

- [ ] Absence of fellowship, support, and security of Christians who love and care (especially for those who became Christians while in the U.S.)
- [ ] Difficulty in finding a good church, which leads to "church hopping"
- [ ] Not being welcomed with open arms in some churches
- [ ] Young people expected to listen and accept what older people say
- [ ] Proof of returnee's commitment to Christ before accepting him into the church
- [ ] Viewed as a threat to the pastor or church leadership
- [ ] Overeagerness to be a part of the church (is ignored or overloaded with work)
- [ ] Judgmental attitude toward church at home in contrast to U.S. church
- [ ] Sharp contrast between clergy and laity
- [ ] Perceived as aggressive, arrogant, critical, whether true or not
- [ ] Difficulty in distinguishing between "Christian" and "American"
- [ ] Limited methods of promoting Christianity
- [ ] Different dynamics in small groups or Bible studies
- [ ] Difficulty in using or applying ministry skills learned in the U.S.
- [ ] Impatience with program, process, or slow production
- [ ] Temptation to feel superior to church leaders who may not have been in the U.S.

As you can see, the returning international student may experience a broad sweep of difficulties. The challenge is to first recognize problems, then plot strategies to handle them. You can help serve as a sounding board for your international friend.

Some Practical Suggestions for Returning Students

1. Find other returnees with whom you can share and have fellowship.

2. Give yourself time to readjust; be patient with yourself and with others.

3. Recognize and accept which transition stage you are going through, and remember that "reverse culture shock" or "reentry shock" is a normal part of the process of returning home.

4. Have a good sense of humor.

5. Let your reentry work for you: use it as a growing process to continue learning about yourself as a bicultural or multicultural person.

6. Appreciate the opportunity you have had to go abroad, and your commitment to return home.

7. Find someone who can give you a current briefing about your community, church, culture, country, job situation, and people you know.

8. Review the most significant changes you have undergone while in the U.S., and the implications of those changes.

9. Review your great expectations in returning home. How relevant and realistic are they?

10. Keep a clear perspective, and remember that God is there with you!

Apply What You Have Learned

1. After reading this chapter, be prepared to help your friend prior to departure. Remember that preparation is the best deterrent to stress.
2. Periodically encourage your student to be in regular contact with loved ones at home through letters, e-mail, fax, or telephone.
3. Discuss with your friend how he or she might be changing during his or her stay in the United States.
4. Prior to the student's departure, discuss the vital elements of this chapter with him or her.

5. Encourage the student by lovingly discussing
   - the positive aspects of their country and home;
   - how he or she can minister to and impact his or her culture positively through his or her newly gained faith, education, and experience;
   - how you can pray for each other during the upcoming transition period.
6. Establish clearly how you can best communicate after he or she has gone home.
7. Purchase a copy of *Think Home* and go through it with your student before they return to their home country.

ELEVEN

Old Ideas and New Ones for Ministry

"A new command I give you: Love one another. As I have loved you, so you must love one another. By this all men will know that you are my disciples, if you love one another."

John 13:34–35

One of the most effective means we have found to minister informally to international students is the Friday night potluck supper. It's a tried-and-true method that we will enlarge upon in this chapter. Another innovative means to touch international students is the information super highway.

A Friday Night Favorite—Potluck

It's a Friday afternoon in Escondido, California. Wichit and Miriam Maneevone are making some preparations for their weekly gathering of international students and friendship partners. Most students enjoy getting away from their classes and studies with a potluck supper. Years ago, the Maneevones were themselves international students in America, and today they have one of the most active ministries to internationals in the nation.

They have been blessed with a large home that comfortably accommodates 30 to 70 students and friendship partners for suppers and meetings. Students arrive from four to six different campuses in the San Diego area. These students are committed to the Friday night gathering. Some will drive 30-45 minutes one way to attend.

Wichit says, "We focus mainly on meeting the needs of the Christian international student, but non-Christians know they are welcome to attend and observe. Most of our students have been drawn to the Lord because of the love among Christians." In the summer of 1987, about one third of the participants were non-Christians, but by the end of the following summer, every one of those who continued were Christians, including a Muslim girl. In 1995-96, eleven students accepted Jesus Christ as their personal Lord and Savior.

The students that attend this gathering are predominately from Pacific Rim countries, but others come from Europe, South America, and Africa. Wichit says, "We find it builds a stronger group when the nationalities are not too diverse, because Christians have a greater chance of bonding here and following up with each other back home. We do not strive to find many nationalities, nor do we try to limit it to one group of people. We just pray for hearts open to learn about Jesus and who are willing to be obedient to his teachings."

Many international student groups meet on Friday evenings around the United States for a potluck supper and general meeting. The Escondido group is one of scores of ISI weekly student meetings across the U.S. It is officially called "International Christian Fellowship," or ICF, as it is commonly known, and was designed as a regular gathering of Christian internationals and Americans for the purpose of learning how to function as the body of Christ. They are intentionally nondenominational and cross-cultural with the desire to help the students grow in worship, Bible study, Christian character, small group leadership, involvement, and stewardship. The ICF wants to help believers experience the Christian life in a practical way and provide a way for non-Christian students to see a living testimony of Christians. It's a safe place for Christian internationals to invite their non-Christian friends and forge new friendships. While Miriam and Wichit Maneevone serve as teachers for the Escondido group, the international students lead the worship and organize the meetings.

Following are guidelines for *your* Friday meetings. You can become a part of ISI's growing ICF network and provide interaction with internationals from various nations.

When and Where

Friday evening is the best time to meet. After a full week of classes, most students are ready to get away from their studies for an evening.

Often they stay late and sleep in the next morning. Saturday night isn't a good choice because it encourages the student to miss church on Sunday. These Friday evening meetings are *not* an alternative to the local church.

There are several location options for the Friday evening meeting, such as various public facilities or a room in a building on campus. The room should be in good condition, and the area should have adequate parking and be within walking distance for the students. The disadvantage in using a public facility is time limitations. Often students like to stay late and unwind after a hard week of studies. Sometimes a church or campus setting doesn't permit a relaxed atmosphere.

A private home is the first choice—either a student apartment or a community member's home. Students feel more freedom to use the kitchen, play games, sing, or even sleep if necessary. The disadvantages of a home are size limitations and possible transportation difficulties. You will need to work out a meeting place that suits your particular situation and availability.

The ICF Friday Schedule

ICF Friday evening meetings include a free dinner. The food is often provided by other U.S. Christians or church groups who take responsibility for an individual Friday night. The fellowship starts about 6:30 P.M. and usually lasts until after midnight. Wichit Maneevone says, "We don't set times for arrival or departure, since this would imply there are times when the students are not welcome. Instead, we let them know when dinner will be served and ask them to turn out the lights when they leave. My wife and I are often asleep before everyone goes home. Sometimes students sleep over."

After a buffet-style supper, which allows students to serve themselves, singing begins around 7:30. Newcomers are introduced, announcements are given, and an offering is taken, followed by more singing. From 8:30 until 10:00, the students have a small-group Bible study. As much as possible, mature international students should take leadership of all aspects of the meeting, including leading the Bible study groups if they are equipped. Finally, refreshments are served, such as tea, coffee, cookies, fresh fruit, and when appropriate, a birthday cake or two. The Maneevones have given themselves permission to go to bed when tired, but Wichit says, "The time of greatest closeness and openness among the students is often between midnight and three in the morning. They will usually discuss serious and personal spiritual issues during this time."

How to Begin Meaningful Friday Evening Meetings

- Pray for the students and their times together.
- Cultivate vision for the overall ministry and share this vision with key Christian international students who will support the meetings.
- Focus your energy on discipling leaders. Give student leaders opportunity to lead as you coach and encourage them in this ministry.
- Don't be discouraged by small numbers. Wichit writes, "We should not be surprised when some we trust and invest our lives in betray us. Be patient and set the example with your own commitment."

Guidelines for New People at the Friday Evening Meetings

- After an international student has attended the meeting two or three times, Wichit makes a follow-up appointment with the student on campus.
- Leaders make sure each student meets three or four other students at the meeting.
- New students fill out a short information card, and then are sent a welcome card.
- Hosts should develop a relationship with the newcomers and help them with their practical needs (i.e., moving, transportation, etc.).

Reasons for Dismissal from the Friday Evening Meeting

It will be rare, but sometimes participants are asked not to return to the meetings. Here are a few possible reasons for dismissal:

- Male students who are looking for a girlfriend and are not trustworthy in relating to the opposite sex.
- Anyone who creates disunity in the meetings by pushing secondary doctrines.
- American college students attending simply for the good food.

- Americans who are not interested in relating to international students.

Friday night potlucks are an ideal way to meet and interact with international students. It could be a first step toward a meaningful friendship. Contact ISI for information on Friday night potlucks in your area, or arrange to host such a regular meeting yourself.

The Cyberspace Connection

About a year ago, one of the ISI staff members attending a welcoming reception in Upper New York State for new International Students, Incorporated staff members spoke briefly at the service but did not sit on the platform. Later that evening at the reception, attended by about 300 people, he noticed a young man sitting alone. Since he was a shy individual himself, he hated to see others sitting alone.

He introduced himself and met Dr. Lim, a forty-year-old medical doctor from China. He was a hearing specialist and had come to the United States for two years of post-doctoral research. As they talked further, the staff person discovered that Dr. Lim had left his wife and family for the time of his studies. He also told him he was a Marxist and an atheist, and had arrived in the United States from China only two days ago. Because Dr. Lim's English was excellent, the staff member inquired how long he had studied English. "Three and a half years," was the response. The church was located several miles from the campus, and the staff person wondered how the doctor had heard of the meeting, having arrived only two days before. When he asked, "How did you find our meeting?" Dr. Lim smiled. "On the Internet," he said. He had found the ISI web page through the cyberspace connection that, for many international students, is answering questions and giving guidance about America long before they set foot on this soil.

Still curious, the staff member asked why Dr. Lim had come to an ISI meeting. "I want to find out about God," he said matter-of-factly. Since that particular meeting, Dr. Lim has been faithfully attending a Bible study almost every week and has since made a commitment to Christ. His wife later joined him and has also become a Christian. Dr. Lim is one of many who come to the United States hungering to know about God. For Dr. Lim, his spiritual journey began on the Internet.

Cyberspace is a new worldwide frontier, and International Students, Incorporated has jumped into the adventure. Millions of computer users are tapping onto the Internet. About half of those users are from the United States, but the other half are from around the globe. Some Christians raise their eyebrows when they hear the word "Internet." They say, "There's pornography on the Internet. The Internet is evil." People criticized the use of television in much the same way when it first came on the market. The Internet is not evil. Though some people may be using it for evil purposes, International Students, Incorporated and other Christian groups are using it for God's purposes.

A Dual Purpose

International Students, Incorporated is an organization that helps Christian volunteers develop friendships with international students and visiting scholars. One purpose of the ISI web page is to educate and inform those who are interested in having an international friend, or in being a friend to internationals.

On the other side of the world, a student is planning to come to the U.S., but he or she may have many questions—which previously remained questions until the student arrived in the U.S. But with the Internet, students can even arrange for someone to meet their plane at the airport. They can also ask questions about

- U.S. etiquette/manners
- purchasing insurance
- learning to drive
- learning about his/her campus, and a multitude of other relevant topics.

They can also request the ISI booklet "How to Survive in the U.S." or receive a copy of the Bible in their own language, or in English, or in both—along with study guides for use with the Bible. Perhaps the international would like to have an American cyber-pal (pen pal on the Internet). Computer literate Christians are matched with internationals through the cyber-pal program.

William, in Taiwan, requested a cyber-pal. He had completed his BS and master's degrees at Arizona State University. Last March he returned home and located a job as a computer programmer for Acer Sertek, a computer corporation. While attending ASU, William had been active in the international student activities, including Bible studies. However, he says, "I was not a Christian. I couldn't believe that God really exists in the world and couldn't understand how so many people could believe in God. I had never seen any miracle that the Bible depicts; therefore, miracles could not happen."

After returning home, and corresponding via e-mail with his Christian cyber-pal, William's ideas about God are beginning to change. He writes, "So many things happened to me after I came home. Difficulties and pains. The pains in my mind were killing me, and I just couldn't get away. I needed Jesus. I found a Presbyterian church that helps me a lot."

The electronic world is only a few keystrokes away from anyone in the world who has a computer, telephone line, and a modem. This program is presently running in ISI, though in its infant stage. The future is bright for a worldwide witness for Christ on the Worldwide Web. You might want to check out the ISI site at: http://www.isionline.org/

Apply What You Have Learned

1. Are you involved in a Friday night potluck to meet and form friendships with international students? If not, how could you get involved? Contact ISI (see Appendix A) to see how you can become a part of it's growing ICF network of student fellowships.
2. You may not have a computer, but you can be involved in worldwide outreach through prayer. Commit to pray for God's guidance with regard to the cyberspace connection for international students and volunteers.
3. If you have a computer, consider logging onto the site and looking around. Check back often as the ISI page is expanded into new areas.
4. Perhaps you would like to be a Christian cyber-pal with an international student. Register by calling 1-800-ISITEAM or e-mail ISI at ISITEAM@aol.com.

TWELVE

A Boost for the Local Church

*"When he saw the crowds, he had compassion on them,
because they were harassed and helpless, like sheep without
a shepherd. Then he said to his disciples, 'The harvest is
plentiful but the workers are few. Ask the Lord of the
harvest, therefore, to send out workers
into his harvest field.'"*

Matthew 9:36–38

As a member of her church missions committee, Kathy Snell was known as the spokesperson for cross-cultural missions. One day, she made an appointment to meet with her pastor to discuss some new energy to pour into their church and missions.

Pastor Willis began the session by saying, "Kathy, I hear you have some new ideas for ministry. Let's hear them."

Reaching into her briefcase, Kathy pulled out a legal pad filled with notes and ideas. "For the last several weeks, I have been noticing how many international students are in our community. What really caught my attention was running into a student from Indonesia who told me there are almost 150 students from his country here, some with families. Our missions committee has been wanting to support the missionary efforts in Indonesia, but we're still looking for the right project or people to do it. It may be a better approach to reach out to international students from Indonesia while they are here, but I'm not sure how to do it."

Pastor Willis agreed. "It's a good idea, but, like you, I don't know exactly how to proceed and organize such a ministry within the church."

Kathy and her pastor discussed how many new ideas for ministry had begun strong but faded within a short period of time. To start an effective ministry for international students within their local church, they needed a comprehensive plan. The difference between a good idea and the implementation of it is in securing adequate information.

International Students, Incorporated has developed a detailed plan for the local church to start a ministry to internationals in their area. Over 1,000 churches have implemented these programs in the nation, and this chapter is built on the cumulative experience of these churches. Through a step-by-step process, we will give an overview of how any church can begin this vital ministry.

The American church is not callous or hardhearted. It has an enormous love for others and gift for missions. But at this point, the church needs to be guided and directed toward that mission field, which is most strategic. David Aikman, former *Time* magazine correspondent to China and one of the men instrumental in Billy Graham's first meetings in China, said, "The 83,000 mainland Chinese students, spouses, and diplomats in the United States are the most strategic evangelistic mission field in the world." And within the reach of virtually every church in America.

How Long Does It Take to Get It Going?

ISI has developed a detailed church ministry manual called *How to Develop an International Student Ministry in Your Church* (see Appendix A for ordering information). There are four phases:

Phase One: Preparing for Ministry (Up to 6+ months) emphasizes the necessity of acquiring a working knowledge of your specific ministry opportunity to international students.

Phase Two: Starting a Ministry (Up to 12+ months) addresses the practical how-to issues of organizing a ministry team and designing a workable ministry strategy and structure.

Phase Three: Building the Ministry (1 to 3+ years) examines how to keep this newly formed outreach moving forward and properly focused by identifying issues that can creep in and derail an unsuspecting ministry.

Phase Four: Maintaining and Renewing the Ministry (3+ years) takes the long-term view about how you can keep your church's ministry vibrant and relevant to both the international students you serve and the volunteers providing the services.

Phase One: Prepare for Ministry

Step One: Agree on Some Fundamental Issues

- Define the ministry focus. Distinguish between God's view and the church's view. This book has promoted the importance of ministry to international students, but the local church will need to reiterate this need. God wants to create a global congregation from every tribe, tongue, and language (Revelation 5:1-6). We've been called to share our faith with international students, and our church has been designed as a community of love to the nations these students represent (Isaiah 56:6-7; Ephesians 2:19).
- Define the ministry focus and what our response should be—prayer. Christians in the local church need to be mobilized for concerted prayer about establishing a ministry to international students. Pray that the Lord will bring volunteers for the key positions in the ministry, such as church coordinator, friendship partner coordinator, international student coordinator, activities coordinator, publicity coordinator, prayer coordinator, and evangelism/discipleship coordinator. Also pray for volunteers within your church who will befriend international students. Pray for the international students. Finally, pray for the church's relationship with the local university or college.

Step Two: Gain Knowledge About What Can Be Done and What Is Being Done

- Obtain information from International Students, Incorporated about materials and staff members in your area. These resources will enable you to start your ministry on a solid foundation.
- Meet with the Foreign Student Adviser (FSA) at the university. FSAs are charged to care for the welfare of international students. Some may be open to volunteer involvement from churches, others may be suspicious. When you call on the local FSA, indicate your personal desire for involvement. The FSA wants someone who genuinely

cares, will meet the needs of international students, won't force his or her religious or personal beliefs on students, and will follow through on commitments.

Your objectives in meeting with the FSA are to

1. establish yourself as someone willing to help meet the needs of international students;

2. determine the international student enrollment;

3. find out what programs are currently offered and who offers them;

4. ask if there is any way you could help as a volunteer.

The FSA may know of services they would like to provide but for which they do not have the people or resources.

If you find FSA tentative or uncooperative, making it difficult to establish any kind of rapport, try to discover the reason for the difficulty. Maybe the last volunteer was a disaster and left a bad taste. Also, seek a common acquaintance who can provide you some credibility with the FSA. This could be a leader in your congregation who is also a business leader in the community or the university. If you are unable to establish rapport with the FSA, ask God to open another door of opportunity. Finally, persevere and prove your willingness to do anything. Small things, such as picking up students at the airport, could lead to greater opportunities. Call ISI for help if the FSA is totally unreceptive.

- Survey existing programs in the community. Are there other programs already in operation, such as conversational English classes? If so, you will want to visit this program to learn how they are meeting the needs of international students. Your purposes at this point are to research and discover any unmet needs in the community or to cooperate with existing programs.

- Survey the resources within your church. How near is your church to the college or university? Are there members of the congregation with campus contacts?

- Visit other communities that have established model programs in their churches. ISI can refer you to situations that will be similar to yours. Take one or two interested people to visit and learn how others have been successful.

- Create a list of the outreach possibilities in an international student ministry. How can your church meet the needs of internationals? (i.e., friendship, providing transportation, providing warm clothing, mentoring, housing assistance).

Step Three: Examine Your Motives for Ministry

We have given you a multitude of motivations for an international student ministry, but a key part of establishing a local church ministry is self-examination. International students are very good at detecting a hidden agenda in our outreach efforts. We've listed some guidelines in this area:

1. Regardless of the activity or program, always give the student complete details of what he can expect. The quickest way to kill your reputation with a university or college is to invite international students to an evangelistic dinner without a clear indication that the program will be religious in nature.

2. Exercise unconditional friendship. Show love to students regardless of their response to you.

3. Remember that the results of any program are in God's hands. Our goal in a church program is to provide an atmosphere in which the Gospel can be effectively shared from our life and testimony.

Step Four: Do Your Homework

Unfortunately, many churches launch an international student ministry only to discover that it is not what the internationals need or that someone else is already providing the same service—and doing it better. Find out what the needs are and then go about trying to fill them. The South Hills Presbyterian Church, just outside of Washington, D.C., was stumped in their international ministry.

Scott Lane, the international ministry team coordinator, had no idea what to do next. The church had a reputation for a proactive involvement in the community with an active membership of 400 families and more than a dozen major ministry programs. They even had a special budget for their international student ministry. Yet this ministry to internationals lacked a personal touch. They had twenty friendship partners matched with international students, but the members in the program didn't have time to meet regularly with the students.

Reverend Mullins encouraged Scott, saying, "This ministry is key for our church, but it's all in the timing. Keep trying!"

Scott took the pastor's encouragement and set up a special brainstorming session with the other international student team members.

They agreed to skip lunch every day for the next week to pray for renewal of the ministry. In addition, the team took their concerns to the entire church, and Scott asked Rev. Mullins to schedule a Sunday evening church presentation.

At the Sunday meeting, Albert, an outgoing Christian student from Malaysia and his friendship partner, Bob, gave a presentation. They began by discussing Albert's difficulties when he first arrived in the United States three years earlier. At a "chance" meeting in a supermarket, Bob and Anne Nicholson invited him to attend an international student meeting at South Hills Presbyterian.

During the interview, Bob paused dramatically and asked Albert, "What would have happened had you not joined our international student ministry?"

Without hesitation, Albert said, "I would have given up and gone home. And I probably would have asked everyone in Malaysia after returning, 'What happened to all the Christians in America?'" Albert continued, "Churches need to help. Students like me need Christian friends, and you can make a difference in our lives." Bob concluded the presentation and explained the simple nature of ministry to international students.

In the weeks after the presentation, Reverend Mullins continued to remind his congregation of the prayer needs of the international student ministry. By the following August, when the ministry team advertised for the fall semester, more than twenty new people volunteered to be friendship partners. Scott was glad he persevered, but waiting for God to move was not easy.

Phase Two: Start a Ministry

Before your church begins a ministry to international students, it's important to determine what needs to be done (phase one) and also to recruit volunteers by telling them about specific needs and opportunities.

Step Five: Define Your Capabilities

- Determine a tentative strategy for your international student ministry. Make sure you temper your plan with realism and don't try to do the impossible. It's better to achieve one well-planned program than four sloppy ones.

- Secure the firm support of the church leadership. This doesn't mean they will necessarily provide "hands-on" help from the pastoral staff, but you do need them to be behind your efforts.

- Arrange a second visit with the FSA to talk about your research and how some people in your church want to be involved. FSAs are usually more comfortable with individuals from the community rather than a church. When you face hesitancy from the FSA, here are three approaches:

    1. The real issue for the FSAs is motivation. Why are you interested in these international students? Explain that as a Christian you are concerned and motivated to reach out to people with love (Leviticus 19:33-34; Romans 12:13).

    2. It is worth mentioning that through your new program international students can experience American culture beyond the university. It gives them a chance to meet and befriend people outside their community. Can you imagine attending Tokyo University and the FSA saying to you, "We're glad you are here, but please don't associate with the Buddhists while you are in our country." Sometimes our biases can be unconsciously extended to others who do not share the same reservations.

    3. Assure the FSA that your intention is not to proselytize the international students, but to simply be their friend with no strings attached. This is our true motivation.

Step Six: Recruit Ministry Team Volunteers

- Begin small enough to maintain top quality. You probably have some idea who will join you in this international outreach. Begin by talking with these people about the findings from your research and inviting them to participate with you. Be sure to screen people carefully, recognizing that hidden agendas, needs, and problems are more easily dealt with through selection than through discipline. Look for people who have proven themselves in their ministry and professions.

- Seek the cooperation of the congregation. Set a date with the church staff to present the ministry to the church.

Step Seven: Get Organized

- Identify a ministry team from your list of potential volunteers.
- Invite the ministry team to an organizational meeting. Your agenda should include at least these three items:

1. Lead the group in creating a purpose statement to define the focus of the ministry. This step helps the ministry team give their own personal stamp of ownership and commitment.

2. Determine the strategies you will use to fulfill your purpose. The prior research will be helpful to this process.

You could sense the excitement in the international student ministry team at Skyline Church. They had gathered to plan their strategies. Carol Robbins, the ministry coordinator, had done an excellent job of gathering data and establishing a strong working relationship with the university foreign student adviser. When the team met, they agreed to implement three ministry strategies: a friendship partner program, an activity each month for the partners and their international friends, and an international Sunday school class.

Unfortunately, the Skyline team didn't establish how often they would meet. Problems began to arise and activities were postponed because the team didn't plan ahead. The international Sunday school class floundered because the ministry team didn't consider the level of interest from Christian international students. They also misjudged the interest of non-Christian internationals matched with church friendship partners. The only program to survive the school year was the friendship partner program. The ministry team sensed they had lost credibility among themselves and the church leadership because they had attempted a larger program than they could carry out with quality. Fortunately, they were quick learners, and the next year they refocused with different results.

3. Determine when you would like to hold a training session for your volunteers. Keep in mind that the best time to recruit and train volunteers is just before the students arrive in the fall.

- Be accountable. Discuss with the church leadership how this can be done. Ideally, the ministry should be incorporated into the missions strategy of the church. One of the most appropriate links to the broader church is through the missions committee.

Step Eight: Train Volunteers—Tools for Outreach

- See the appendix to order resources, and contact ISI for help with training your volunteers.

- Training volunteers and coordinators sounds like a major undertaking, but keep in mind that you can receive training from ISI.

Step Nine: Implementing Outreach Plans

- Friendship partners. This program is the most common outreach strategy. International students are matched to church members. The friendship partners agree to meet with their student once each month and to make some kind of weekly contact by phone or a note to keep in touch.
- Professional partners. This program links students with professionals in your church whose career interests and professional specialities match the students'. The details of implementing this program are found in the next chapter.
- There are a multitude of other creative possibilities, one being the regular Friday night International Christian Fellowship (ICF) potluck and meeting, highlighted in the last chapter. You may want to form a group of conversational partners who can help international students with their English skills. A ministry to the spouses of international students is another possible outreach. The key is selecting a program that can be accomplished consistently.

Here Today . . . Gone Tomorrow

Betty James was always looking for things to do within her church. A vibrant, energetic lady, she preferred a hands-on approach to tasks. When challenged with the idea of international student ministry, Betty embraced it wholeheartedly.

Before long, she single-handedly recruited seven couples to be friendship partners. Her pastor was enthusiastic, so he encouraged her to continue the outreach. In fact, the pastor wished he had more people in his church like Betty who could see a need and fill it.

Soon her friendship partners were matched with students. Some of these students Betty met in the grocery store, others signed up for an American partner at the college. The new friendship partners enjoyed their relationships with the students. For encouragement, Betty planned a Christmas party. The Chinese students were overwhelmed with the warmth and love from the Christians. It was a completely new experience for them. Each received a gift from their American friend, learned about the true meaning of Christmas, and at the end laughed together when a Chinese student made a surprise showing in a Santa suit.

During the first year, thanks to Betty's hard work, the ministry progressed. Betty made plans to double the ministry the next fall, but it didn't double. There was no Christmas party organized for the Chinese students and, in fact, there was little evidence in the church of a ministry to international students. In June, to Betty's surprise, her husband, Frank, was transferred to a new location. Though the church had been thrilled with Betty's ministry to internationals, there was no accountability between her and the broader church. Because she was doing such a good job, no one thought to interfere or inquire how things were done. Consequently, when Betty left the church, the ministry folded. She had not been responsible in preparing for her replacement and in structuring a long-term ministry for the church. If a ministry team is well organized, with plenty of group participation, it can survive the loss of its leader. But in this case the church's ministry to international students was here today and gone tomorrow.

Phase Three: Build the Ministry

Step Ten: Review the Operation

After your outreach is underway, seek regular feedback from the church volunteers and internationals at regular intervals. Document the feedback and use the information to make adjustments in your program. The first time is always a learning experience. You will find that some things work well one year and "bomb" the next. For example, you may find that your volunteers are insensitive to the school academic schedule. Many times churches plan a big Christmas program during finals week on campus.

Step Eleven: Communicate and Continue Education

- Keep volunteers and friendship partners informed through newsletters, announcements in the church bulletin, and informal gatherings for encouragement.
- Keep everyone in the congregation informed. Continue to keep prayer needs and ministry needs before the entire church. Encourage the pastor to pray for the ministry once a month and to share special prayer needs with the Sunday school classes.

- Prepare a ministry that lasts for the long-term. Recruit and train replacements for every position so the ministry isn't dependent on a single individual.

- Prepare for changes in your ministry. As the ministry progresses, the questions will also change. For example, initial questions might include: "What kind of food do I prepare for internationals?" and "Will I be able to communicate with them?" Later, the questions will change to: "How do I know if they are interested in the Gospel?" or "My student is Muslim; how can I tell him about Christ in a way he can understand?" See Appendix A for additional resources to help answer these changing questions.

- Maintain meaningful team meetings for prayer and planning. Each church and group dynamic is different. You will need to determine the frequency of the meetings for your situation, but be aware of three common errors with these types of meetings:

1. Don't meet *too* frequently (so everyone tires of meetings).

2. Meet frequently enough (so you are not in danger of losing touch).

3. Don't meet when you don't need to meet (team members will feel they are wasting time).

Necessity—the Mother of Invention

The friendship partner program at Covenant Baptist Church was flourishing. Coordinator Pat Riley was enthusiastic about her two-year investment. She had effectively recruited and trained volunteers and kept in contact through regular social activities and a monthly newsletter. She established a regular follow-up for the friendship partners to share their struggles and experiences with her volunteer prayer group. Over the past year, seven international students had committed their lives to Jesus Christ—four Asian students, two Africans, and one European. Little did Pat know that the blessing of these eager new Christians would turn into a personal struggle.

Pat had given little thought to the steps beyond friendship and evangelism—namely discipleship and integration into the local church. She learned also that the friendship partners knew little about discipleship. They had taken their international student friends to church but it had not worked out well. The Asians seemed disinterested (later they said they had a hard time following the fast-talking pastor), and the Africans were bogged down by the music. These international students didn't fit into either the home builders or the college Sunday school classes.

None of these friendship partners had ever helped a new believer grow in his faith—neither did they feel qualified to begin learning with an international Christian. As Pat thought about integrating the students into the church, she felt badly about not having planned ahead. Even the social activities for internationals had taken place in natural settings outside the church. "They're islands sitting out there," Pat said. "How can I build these students into a community, into an international Christian fellowship?"

Pat called upon some staff members at International Students, Incorporated to learn how to follow up with new believers. They gave her some solid suggestions, then guided her through the next steps. They suggested the following:

- Begin a new Sunday school class within the church, a cross-cultural Bible class with joint fellowship time, then electives to meet the students' specific needs.
- Look within the church for mature Christians gifted in the areas of discipleship or cross-cultural ministry.
- Survey your friendship partners to determine what ministry gifts they have among them. Can some of them teach a Bible study? Show hospitality? Explain how to live out one's faith through one's vocation?
- Locate mature Christian internationals from the community or campus to help.
- Learn about cross-culturally sensitive discipleship resources from ISI and elsewhere to help the friendship partners be effective in discipleship and studying the Bible with their international friends.

A year later, with the help of two mature church members, Pat has seen several of the new Christians fit into their cross-cultural Sunday school class. They are becoming a part of the church body also—even to the point of serving others in some of the church's programs and ministries. Pat is very pleased about having a more balanced ministry for outreach and discipleship to international students. Necessity was the mother of invention at Covenant Baptist Church.

Phase Four: Maintain and Renew the Ministry

Prayer, communication, and fellowship are themes that run throughout the ministry of the local church. As your ministry to international students makes use of these three resources, the ministry will have a vital role in your local church. This final phase is critical for the continuation and growth of the ministry.

Step Twelve: The Church Link: Does Your Church Embrace the International Student Ministry?

Continually invest in the relationship between the church and the international student ministry. Your link should be maintained in the following areas:

- Service. You are serving the church with international student ministry, but the ministry is also serving the needs of the church and its members. A life of service is best learned when modeled in the context of the local church and its outreach to the community.
- Support. Prayer, financial, and manpower support are the tangible expressions of how the ministry functions within the church and also determines its importance. If you need anything in one or more of these three areas (prayer, financial, manpower), don't be afraid to ask—provided you have served in these areas first.
- Accountability. When the church leadership asks, "How's the ministry going?" it represents more than a greeting. It is a question about the use of God's resources, and it provides an opportunity to talk about God's blessing and work in your midst.
- Commitment. The quality of your relationship with the church depends on the depth of your commitment. Be as committed to the health of your church as you are to the ministry.

Step Thirteen: Keeping the Vision for Ministry Alive

Your international student ministry runs on gallons of clear vision. The ministry vision needs systematic restatement, clarification, and communication within the ministry team and the church. It is the guiding result, inspiration, and focus of the ministry.

- Vision. A vision statement is a brief, clear description of the result that the ministry intends to achieve. It tells why the ministry exists and what it intends to accomplish.
- Restatement and clarification. The vision statement should be consistently repeated until everyone understands clearly what you are doing, as well as what you are not doing. It's probably not possible

to repeat the vision statement too frequently.

- Communication. Each member of the ministry needs to be given an opportunity to demonstrate a basic understanding of the vision. This vision is maintained and kept alive when people see us moving steadily toward the accomplishment of the vision. Communication is critical.
- Identity. The vision also tells us who we are as a ministry. It affects our values, the ends we seek, and the means we choose to accomplish those ends.
- Focus and direction. Vision points us toward our goal and warns us of distractions along the way. Without a clear vision, there are no real priorities to guide our activities.

Step Fourteen: Generating Team Work—the Personal Touch

Great teamwork isn't magic. It requires much effort on the part of the leader. Your team members will stay encouraged when they know they are cared for, appreciated, and assured they are making a significant contribution to the ministry.

- Hard work. It takes hard work to care for international students, but it also takes work to care for the friendship partners and volunteers. Every member of the team is important.
- Care. Team members need to know they are valued as individuals and not only for their productivity on a task.
- Appreciation and significance. Merely saying "thank you" is a powerful way to encourage your team in their specific personal contributions. The fact that you recognize what God is doing through their roles in the ministry is critical to their perception of their value to the ministry. If people do not feel they are contributing significantly, they will take their efforts elsewhere. On the other hand, enthusiasm is contagious when team members fully understand their part in the total ministry picture.

Step Fifteen: Training—Keeping Up the Pace

A major challenge for international student ministry leaders is to continually help their team members grow and to equip them with new tools for the task. Good training will increase the capacity of your team to serve and will deepen their commitment to the ministry. As you give time and attention to training the team, it will enable them to be more effective and productive.

- Growth. As your team grows spiritually, intellectually, and interpersonally, it will result in a dynamic ministry. We are stretched outside of our comfort zones through a variety of experiences.
- Training. Increased training will build the personal confidence and effectiveness of the ministry team. International Student Ministry volunteers and friendship partners will want to become associates with ISI, be in the ISI communications loop, and receive the same training opportunities as ISI staff for regional and national training conferences (see Appendix A for associate information).
- Freedom. Well-trained people will feel free to initiate within their sphere of ministry.

Step Sixteen: Stop, Look, and Listen—Reevaluating

If you expect to maintain momentum in international student ministry, regular reassessment and reflection on the quality of your ministry is essential. Are you asking the right questions? Why are you doing this ministry? What are the results? How could it be done better? Are you still having fun? There is always data for evaluation, but the challenge is to study the data and learn from both mistakes and successes. Then you will be progressively doing things better.

- Reassessment and reflection. An old Chinese proverb says, "Unless we change direction, we are likely to end up where we are headed." Looking back and forward is a time-consuming yet crucial process to maintaining and renewing ministry.
- Evaluation of the data. There are many ways to measure a successful ministry. One of the critical methods is observing people's responses to our efforts. Ask pertinent questions and do periodic follow-up to give you the necessary information for good ministry decisions. The natural tendency in established ministries is to assume that our years of experience allow us the luxury of making assumptions—without ever questioning their accuracy.
- The challenge. It takes concentration and courage to analyze our past efforts and continually improve. For the ministry to stay vital and fresh, we must take this step. Without it, a ministry loses touch with the needs and priorities of its constituents.

Step Seventeen: Stay in Touch with Returnees

Your commitment to international students should be characterized by the statement "Out of sight but *not* out of mind." Someday, the majority of these students will be returning home. You can help them prepare for reentry into their home cultures and then keep in contact with them after they arrive home. This connection will secure a lifeline of friendship, fellowship, and encouragement.

- Reentry preparation. See chapter 11 to help your student prepare for returning home.
- Contact. As a student readjusts to his own culture, it helps immensely to have a friend who understands.
- Lifeline. With many international friends, we can provide encouragement and perspective. For Christian returnees, we are spiritual partners to support their faith and walk with Christ. Our prayers may make the difference in a long-term impact on their home cultures.
- Students who do not want to return. Occasionally, students will seek help from their friendship partner to stay in the United States. This creates a dilemma for the American, the student's government, and the U.S. government. Despite your love for the student, any decision should be the result of concerted prayer and counsel with the local ISI staff member and the student's Foreign Student Adviser.

Step Eighteen: Strengthening the Partnership With the Campus

As your ministry with international students matures, it can be a significant source of help to the university. Cooperation with the international student office can result in meeting more students. The welcome mat may be kept out for you if you are faithful in identifying common goals and working together with the FSA to meet the needs of international students.

- Cooperation. We must not compromise our purpose but seek to discover where we can serve each other—areas where we agree and our goals coincide. Mutual trust, which is established over time, is the result of sensitive listening to the concerns of each party and faithfulness in doing what was promised. This area requires personal and interpersonal maturity, so be careful who represents your ministry in this area.
- Meeting needs. As Christians, we seek to serve a wide range of human

needs: physical, intellectual, social, and spiritual. Internationals are not exempt. A maturing ministry keeps a good balance in all of these areas and teaches everyone involved in the ministry how to work in each area.

Step Nineteen: Increase Service by Termination/Expansion

Programs and services that meet student needs require regular maintenance and updating. Eliminate unnecessary aspects and add more strategic dimensions of ministry. Find out from the internationals what their greatest needs are and then create a new approach to serve them. A carefully planned expansion effort will bring renewal, balance, and quality to your ministry.

- Fine-tuning and updating. Because something worked well at one time or with one group does not mean it will continue to work well. We need to ask ourselves, "Are we currently meeting the most important student needs?" Find out definitively. The discovery process and response to the results will bring excitement to your students, volunteers, and ministry team.
- Renewal. "New and improved" is not merely a marketing technique. It is necessary to keep a ministry alive and growing. Within every ministry that pursues excellence, there is room for improvement. Adding new aspects to the ministry will usually mean adding new people. This process alone adds a renewing agent: the questions novices ask.

Don't Become Overwhelmed

Nineteen steps to a vital international student ministry in your church could seem a bit overwhelming to the uninitiated. Instead, we hope you will see these steps as a beacon of light that can guide you to effective ministry in the local church. Thousands of churches have followed these steps and you can join them in this important service to these strategic future leaders.

Getting It Together by Getting Together

Cheryl Nelson had her hands full as the church international ministry team coordinator for the international student ministry. Their suburban church of 600 members had 25 friendship partners. Her husband, Phil, was taking adult education classes at a nearby community college where 250 international students attended. His contact with these students and a guest speaker at their church sparked the Nelsons' involvement in the ministry.

However, two years into their ministry, they started to lose many of their friendship partners. After evaluation, they discovered that many of them felt left alone—not sure what to do, and lacking support and confidence. Several suggested getting together to discuss particular issues and problems facing friendship partners.

The Nelsons began hosting a monthly gathering of friendship partners and volunteers to encourage everyone in the ministry. Because the meetings were informal, the participants felt free to talk about their personal needs, and a strong sense of community began to develop. At each meeting, people shared prayer requests and personal needs as well as highlights and disappointments in their relationships with international students. These meetings also served as a forum to share ideas and discuss issues relating to the international student ministry. As a result of these meetings, everyone took a greater interest and pride in the ministry. They felt like a part of a team.

Occasionally, the Nelsons invited someone to the group who was experienced in cross-cultural relationships—either Christian international students or Americans involved in international relationships or studies. At one meeting, a couple who had recently returned from missionary work with youth in Japan discussed how to befriend and share the Gospel with Japanese youth. At another meeting, the group studied ISI training materials on how to initiate conversations on spiritual matters with their international friends.

During these meetings, the Nelsons quickly discovered that one of the major obstacles facing most of the friendship partners was getting beyond friendship into witnessing. Finally, the group decided to simply ask their international friends if they would be interested in being involved in a Bible study. Surprisingly, several students were eager to begin. It was almost as if they were waiting to be asked.

As a result, the Nelsons recruited a church member to teach introductory Bible lessons. In turn, the students began asking friendship partners about spiritual issues brought up in these studies, and many students began attending the church. ISI encouraged the use of *Trio*, an easy-to-use evangelistic and basic Bible study (see Appendix A for ordering information).

The Nelsons faced another obstacle after Phil stopped taking classes at the college: a lack of support from the foreign student office. Cheryl began to look for ways to support and serve the office to win their trust and cooperation.

The college's annual international student dinner provided an excellent opportunity. Cheryl and the ministry partners volunteered to prepare shish kabobs. A group of ministry partners and students were mobilized to marinate, prepare, and cook the meat and vegetables on a stick for the event. This group effort impressed the foreign student office and opened the door to further joint activities and access to the students.

This particular group discovered how to improve their international student ministry by increased communication and greater participation.

Apply What You Have Learned

1. Where is your local church in relation to starting a ministry for international students?
2. If there isn't a ministry, how can you take some steps to start one?
3. Who in your church has a heart for missions and/or been on a short-term missions trip? Invite them to a discussion meeting with regard to beginning an international student ministry.
4. Using the guidelines in this chapter, begin your ministry.
5. As a church international student ministry group, become an affiliate with ISI for further help and support (see Appendix A for affiliate information).

THIRTEEN

Mentor a Leader

"He appointed twelve—designating them apostles—that they might be with him and that he might send them out to preach."

Mark 3:14

"Whatever you have learned or received or heard from me, or seen in me—put it into practice. And the God of peace will be with you."

Philippians 4:9

One day, Austin, Texas stockbrokers Robert Berryman and Bob Sims began meeting with an international student couple on a professional level about portfolio management. It started an important relationship. Chen and Lin, both MBA students at the University of Texas, hungered for some practical and real-life instruction beyond what they could reap in a classroom setting.

Their initial meeting for this mentoring relationship centered around different aspects of the business. The more time they spent together, the more Chen asked himself why these two successful businessmen would make time in their busy schedules for him and his wife—especially when they could have used the hours for making money.

Finally Chen mustered the courage to ask why they were making such a sacrifice. His question provided these two business partners an opportunity to share about their Christian values and worldview, which drive all their business practices.

"We got to share how you can plan and implement the most brilliant of strategies . . . but how, ultimately, it is God who controls people and the world's economy," says Sims.

"Also, we got to talk about the fear and greed that drive many people who don't know God and try to make big money short-term in the market," adds Berryman. "We shared by contrast how we make ethical decisions based on the truth of God's Word."

Soon this mentoring relationship blossomed into a cultural exchange and afforded opportunities for Robert and Bob to open their homes to Chen and Lin. With a firm foundation of unconditional friendship, the new friends talked often and openly of spiritual things. Chen and Lin confirmed that they had already made commitments to Christ.

As Chen's studies drew to a conclusion, Berryman and Sims helped him prepare his resumé and gear up for his upcoming interview with Goldman-Sachs. The firm quickly discerned what an asset Chen would be and offered him a prestigious slot on their team in Asia.

Before he left the United States, Chen thanked Berryman and Sims profusely for their input into his life, and asked what he could do to repay the debt he felt he owned them. They said, "Do for someone else what the Lord has done through us for you. That's all the repayment we ask."

The Commitment From a Professional

International Students, Incorporated has a program for professionals called Professionals in Partnership. The professionals who enroll in the program are committed to initiating and cultivating a friendship for at least one year with an international student or visiting scholar who has an interest in their professional field. The friendship provides an opportunity for an international student to learn about the various perspectives on life in a given profession. It is a wonderful way for a professional to build a friendship on his own turf and an opportunity to share the relevance of his Christian faith to his life and work. Likely, there are also ways beyond one's profession to practically assist an international partner.

The Opportunities and Benefits

As a professional partner, you entrust your professional insights and personal perspectives to an international professional who will impact his or her country as a future leader in your field.

You are also able to impart the best values that you and your profession offer to an international partner who is eager for your insights and friendship. Also, you model professionalism to your international friend who respects your professional accomplishments. You will be able to show him or her how to pursue wisdom as well as knowledge, to cultivate character as well as achievements, to value generosity and service above personal gain.

The professional partner ministry has a flexible friendship agenda that will dovetail with your professional goals and also acknowledge the constraints of your personal schedule. Beyond the professional satisfaction, this program allows you to put your faith into practice and provide lifelong benefits to people from the other side of the globe whom you may never otherwise meet.

Professional partners are not limited to doctors and lawyers. A broad gamut of professionals are involved in this program.

How to Get Started

"Mentoring" is a buzz word for the nineties. Many students are looking for a mentor, and you can be that mentor for an international student by being a professional partner. First, fill out an application from International Students, Incorporated. ISI will search for or help you find a student in your area who is studying to go into your profession.

First Contact and First Meeting

After you have been matched in a Professionals in Partnership relationship, you will be expected to make the first call to your international partner. Despite his or her eagerness to hear from you, as a guest in the United States it may seem improper for him or her to call you. In fact, even after the initial meeting it will remain primarily your responsibility to initiate continued contact. During the first call to the international partner, be sure to identify yourself. Explain how you acquired the student's or scholar's name and other details.

We recommend that you make arrangements for your first meeting within two weeks after your first phone call. If your international partner is new to the area, you may wish to arrange to give him or her a ride to the meeting place. Select a meeting location that will best suit both of your schedules: your home or office, a restaurant, or a site on campus. If your new friend is a bit late, don't be discouraged. People from other countries are frequently less time-conscious than Americans.

Your first meeting is a chance for you and your international partner to get acquainted, to learn a little about each other, and hopefully to establish the foundation for a long-lasting and mutually beneficial relationship. Suggest a meeting place that will allow both of you to be comfortable and one that will afford the opportunity to talk casually.

Some ideas for your first meeting might include the following:

- a visit to the campus and a meeting with your student and his or her adviser;
- a brief tour of your office and place of employment;
- taking your international partner to a professional association meeting you regularly attend;
- lunch or dinner in a restaurant;
- inviting your international friend to your home for a meal and to meet your family.

What to Talk About

The primary goal of your first meeting is to begin building a relationship based on truth and friendship. Ask about your international partner's family, how he or she became involved in your profession, and perhaps what courses he or she is enrolled in. Ask educated questions about his or her home country, and discover what a professional lifestyle is like in that part of the world. It is important, however, that you don't pry or try to force a conversation. More guidelines about things to discuss are suggested in chapter 5.

Be a good listener, but also allow your international partner to get to know you as well. Offer helpful information about yourself without dominating the conversation. Use this time to begin sharing perspectives on your profession. Remember that your international partner enrolled in this program out of a shared professional interest and a desire to learn from your experience and insights. Meeting this goal should be your central focus as you begin your relationship. Later, as you spend more time together, your relationship will likely grow beyond the professional aspect into more of a personal friendship.

Here are some suggestions for beginning discussions related to your mutual professional interests:

- Focus on personal character traits, ethics, and values that play a major role in your professional life.
- Discuss career paths, office politics, dealing with interpersonal conflict, and—if you have a family—explore how your family fits into your career.
- Allow for an exchange of perspectives. Although your international partner may not have your depth of experience, he or she can add insight as to how his or her culture perceives and values your profession, enabling you to gain a sharper professional worldview. This interchange will give you an improved understanding of another culture, and it will give your friend a positive view of American professionals.

Helping in Practical Ways

Perhaps there is something that only you can offer your international partner, especially if he or she is a student. You can allow your international friend to see, experience, and learn the aspects of your profession that you would have like to have known before you entered the field. There is valuable information in every field that can only be gained from experience.

- Invite your international partner to spend a day with you on the job. After a brief tour, allow him or her to follow you around to observe your work, or arrange for colleagues to share various aspects of your profession. Include your friend as a silent partner in meetings or during appointments.
- Provide your international partner with copies of professional journals or other related magazines to which you subscribe.
- Use your friends and network to expose your international partner to cutting-edge ideas, processes, and other aspects of your profession.
- Discuss specific skills and competencies your international partner wishes to develop. Together, make a plan of action to address each skill or competency.

Cultivate Your Friendship

Other sections in this book give detailed suggestions for increasing your friendship with your international partner. As you get to know your new friend, you will probably discover some common interests besides the obvious professional ones. Even if it is only a shared appreciation for fine food or music, that can be another solid building block as you cultivate your friendship.

Cross-Cultural Awareness

Culture shapes the way we go about our profession and daily routines. Most international students and visiting scholars come from cultures very different from our own. Accordingly, our perceptions are likewise different. Cultural differences can show up in simple things, such as punctuality, or complex matters, such as speaking with frankness versus being polite by speaking indirectly. These differences can add intrigue and also a little frustration. Other sections in this book highlight the need for cross-cultural awareness. You will need to have these matters in mind as you relate to your international partner.

Not Alone

As you develop your friendship with your international partner, you will want to move the relationship in a spiritual direction. Other chapters in this book will give you insight and helpful guidelines for this process.

Through your professional partnership, you are not alone. Rather, you've joined a nationwide network of thousands of volunteers and ISI staff who are dedicated to this strategic ministry. ISI is committed to helping you be successful in your relationship and ministry to the student or scholar.

Apply What You Have Learned

1. What is your profession? Could you mentor an international student as a professional partner?
2. What steps could you take to initiate this process (i.e., find out what resources are available, contact ISI for an enrollment form, etc.)?
3. What personal benefits and blessings can you see in working with a professional partner?
4. Are there others you could encourage to get involved in such a program? (see Appendix A for resources and information).

FOURTEEN

Join a Large National Movement

*"Woe to me!' I cried. 'I am ruined! For I am a man of
unclean lips, and I live among a people of unclean lips,
and my eyes have seen the King, the LORD Almighty.' Then
one of the seraphs flew to me with a live coal in his hand,
which he had taken with tongs from the altar. With it he
touched my mouth and said, 'See, this has touched your
lips; your guilt is taken away and your sin atoned for.' Then
I heard the voice of the Lord saying, 'Whom shall I send?
And who will go for us?' And I said, 'Here am I. Send me!' "*

Isaiah 6:5–8

*"Of Zebulun, such as went forth to battle, expert in war,
with all instruments of war, fifty thousand, which could
keep rank: they were not of double heart."*

1 Chronicles 12:33, KJV

What an opportunity! In our nation, 554,000 international students need a friend! Can we meet this challenge? Absolutely!

If one half of one percent of all Christians who say they know Jesus Christ as Lord and Savior in a personal way became friendship partners, we would have a friend for every international student in the nation. Christians in our country are not callous. They simply do not know this wonderful mission field exists.

God is sovereign. He knows. God also knows those he has prepared for this wonderful mission opportunity, who are waiting for the chance to minister internationally. The 554,000 volunteers can easily be trained through the ISI Volunteer Kit. God has already prepared them in evangelism. They have a heart for discipleship. Are *you* one of these people?

If you are, your first step is to contact ISI. You can work at any level you desire. Many are needed at every level. The mission field is "white unto harvest" and ready for laborers.

After reading this book, you know that a fulfilling and thrilling opportunity to reach beyond your borders in a way that is comfortable for you is a real possibility. You will be able to love someone for Christ's sake who is in need of your love and of God's love and who will return that love. What a wonderful personal and spiritual relationship can develop!

There are a variety of service levels:

- volunteer friendship partner
- coordinator for a group in your local church
- mobilizer of other people and other churches in your city
- associate with ISI
- part-time helper with ISI
- full-time ISI staff

Be a pioneer in this most strategic of all mission fields. Be a foreign missionary on your own doorstep! Love an international, a future leader of our world, for Christ's sake—without learning another language. Touch someone who will impact others—perhaps a nation, perhaps the world.

Reach the unreached while they are here in our country. Join the most reproductive mission in the world—the international student outreach of love and hospitality.

Peng, from the southeastern corner of the People's Republic of China, now with a Ph.D. in electrical engineering, said after six years in the U.S., "For six months after coming here, I was totally alone and deeply depressed. Then I met someone from ISI, and he introduced me to my best friend, Jesus Christ. Now I am going home to tell my country how to know God." Each of us can be such a friend and help change our world.

Appendix A

Be a part of the movement—join the ISI team as an affiliate or an associate.

Since 1953, God has blessed International Students, Incorporated as a forerunner of ministry to international students. There are two methods of joining hands with ISI:

- Affiliates are churches or organizations linked with ISI.
- Associates are individuals who formalize their relationship with ISI.

Benefits for Affiliates or Associates

Discounts on Materials

As an ISI affiliate or associate you will enjoy generous discounts on materials, purchasing them at cost well below that offered to the general public. These materials include:

- The *Jesus* film, available in many languages
- Foreign language Bibles
- Country and religion profiles
- Training materials
- And much more!

Prayer Network

ISI affiliates and associates are added to our intercessor network as well as our monthly staff prayer list. As a part of the ISI family, affiliates and associates also receive our in-house family communiqué, which shares information and ministry stories from staff, affiliates, and associates around the country.

Toll-Free Phone Consultation

A special ISI affiliate and associate toll-free telephone service allows you instant access to ISI's international student ministry specialist. Simply dial 1–800–ISI–TEAM, to set up your associate or affiliate status.

United States Transfer Network

International students often move from one city to another. Because of the breadth of ISI ministry contacts, ISI can help you find a Christian niche in a new location where your student can find opportunities for fellowship and growth.

Global Follow-Up Network

ISI's Global Follow-up Network will help you connect your international students with other vibrant Christians and returnees when they go back to their home country.

Affiliate and Associate Conferences

To provide continued training, you will be specially invited to attend ISI's regularly scheduled National and Regional Conferences at a discounted rate. At these conferences, you will interact with ISI field team members from across the country as well as meet other international student ministry leaders.

Speaker's Bureau

ISI experts are available to assist your church or organization in developing your international student ministry.

On-Site Visits

ISI stands ready to have expert consultants make on-site visits (at cost) for training, strategic planning, and the evaluation of new and existing ministries.

On-Line Computer Connections

For affiliates and associates who are active on one of the on-line services, ISI is developing a resource section on the Internet, including on-line ministry forums, an idea exchange, on-line conferencing that will link you with others in ministry worldwide, and access to new materials being field tested.

To affiliate or associate with International Students, Incorporated, contact:

International Students, Inc.
P.O. Box C
Colorado Springs, CO 80901
Phone: (719) 576-2700
Fax: (719) 576-5363
Toll-free: 1–800–ISI–TEAM
E-mail: ISITEAM@aol.com

Resources From International Students, Incorporated

Country Profiles

Each country profile contains loads of interesting facts on the culture and customs of the top student-sending nations to the United States. It is a great help for Americans who want to know more about the home country of an international student.

Titles Available:

The People's Republic of China
Japan
Taiwan
India
South Korea
Malaysia
Hong Kong
Indonesia
Pakistan
Thailand

Religion Profiles

These succinct, comprehensive guides provide an overview of a religion or religious issue and evangelistic pointers. They also detail how each religion compares with Christianity.

Topics Available:

Animism
Marxism
Judaism and the Jewish People
Shinto
Is Jesus the Only Way to God?
How Can I Know the Bible is the Word of God?
Islam
Hinduism
Buddhism
Secularism
World Religions Overview
The Compact Guide to World Religions by Dean C. Halverson, General Editor (Bethany House Publishers).

Witnessing Tool

Knowing God Personally: A witnessing tool designed for use with internationals students, stressing our relationship with a personal God (tract/booklet).

Booklets

ISI's series of foundational booklets for American Christians involved in international student ministry. Each booklet is designed for use with a specific people group or to address a unique need. These booklets share helpful cultural and spiritual insights for a more effective witness with your international friend.

Titles available:

How to Share the Good News With Your International Friend
How to Share the Good News With Your Muslim Friend
Reaching Students From the People's Republic of China
How to Share the Good News With Your African Friend
How to Share the Good News With Your Japanese Friend

How to Study the Bible With Your International Friend
Becoming a Friend With an International Student
An American Friend Handbook: A helpful guide for American Christians who desire to befriend international students.
How to Survive in the U.S.: A Handbook for Internationals: A practical cultural guide for newly-arrived students.
Let's Talk About It: A guide to leading pre-evangelistic discussion. Basics of beginning a relationship with an international student.
Churches in Mission With ISI: From a pastor's point of view, shares the value for the local congregation of getting involved in world missions in your own backyard through international student ministry.

Getting Started With the ISI Volunteer Kit (includes a number of printed materials not otherwise available to the public). This helpful kit contains all you'll need to begin a relationship with your international student, including:

- *Getting Started With ISI* (video)
- *Sharing God's Love, Changing the World* (booklet)
- *Knowing God Personally* (witnessing tool tract)
- plus several other items to acquaint you more thoroughly with ISI's ministry and resources.

Other Videos

New Beginnings, which covers the basics of the Christian life in fifteen-minute segments covering: Salvation, Assurance, Lordship, the Bible, Prayer, the Holy Spirit, and Witnessing.

Appendix B
Additional Topics for
Discussion Starters

The following pages include some examples of topics and related questions for discussion parties. Each topic poses a particular question for discussion. You will want to adapt these ideas for your use, or create your own topics and questions.

The Nature of Truth

Is truth relative, absolute, or both? What is the difference between absolute and relative truth? Where can absolute truth be found? Where can relative truth be found?

How has the concept of truth changed during the course of your life? What has caused this?

In what ways has living in a different culture been of value to you in looking for the truth?

What truths do you think are commonly understood in various cultures?

What do you consider to be the most important truth in life?

The Nature of God

How would you describe God?

How would the God you have just described indicate his interest, if any, in individuals?

Would God hear and answer prayers? What examples do you have to indicate that God does or does not respond to prayer?

In what ways has God revealed himself to people, if, in fact, he has done so?

What is your reaction to Blaise Pascal's statement, "Man has a God-shaped vacuum that only God can fill"?

The Meaning of Freedom

What is your response to the statement: "Freedom equals the absence of all restraints?"

What are some different kinds of freedoms?

What pressures or demands interfere with an individual's personal freedom?

If one lives in a country where political freedom is limited, to what extent can one have personal freedom?

What is the relationship between personal freedom and such conditions as physical or financial security?

What steps can an individual take to experience more personal freedom?

What Is Sin?

Note: This topic should only be used in a group that has been very open in discussing other topics and one in which the members have indicated an interest in discussing "sin" as a topic.

How would you define "sin"?

Give some examples of what you would call "sin."

Why, in your opinion, do people sin?

What do you believe is the worst sin?

What is the solution to sin?

Finally, here are some other general topics for discussion. If used, more detailed questions than those listed above will need to be developed:

How do we deal with disappointments?

What are the possible solutions to world hunger?

Success: What is it and how can it be measured?

Science or God as related to the source of hope.

The role of government in a society.

React to the statement: All religions lead to the same God.

How can we have peace in the world?

Which is more important: the well-being of the group, or the well-being of the individual?

What should be our attitude toward the care of natural resources?

Morals: relative or absolute?

What is man's purpose and ultimate destiny?

Notes

Chapter 4

1. George Barna, *The Index of Leading Spiritual Indicators, Trends in Morality, Beliefs, Lifestyles, Religious and Spiritual Thought, Behavior, and Church Involvement* (Dallas: Word Publishing Company, 1996), p. 71.
2. Dean C. Halverson, General Editor. *The Compact Guide to World Religions—Understanding and Reaching Followers of Islam, Buddhism, Hinduism, Taoism, Judaism, Secularism, The New Age, and Other World Faiths* (Minneapolis: Bethany House Publishers, 1996).
3. Patrick Johnstone, *Operation World—The Day-by-Day Guide to Praying for the World* (Grand Rapids, Mich.: Zondervan Publishing House, 1993).
4. Joseph C. Aldrich, *Lifestyle Evangelism* (Sisters, Ore.: Multnomah Press, 1978), p. 209.

Chapter 6

1. L. Robert Kohls, Ph.D., "The Values Americans Live By," unpublished paper, 1988.

Chapter 7

1. *Knowing God Personally*, International Students, Inc., 1995. Original material taken from *Knowing God* by Billy Graham Evangelistic

Association. Scripture references used in tract are taken from The *Holy Bible, New International Version*, 1973, 1978, 1984, International Bible Society; *The Message*, Eugene Peterson, 1993; *The Living Bible*, 1971, Tyndale House Publishers; *The New American Standard Bible*, 1977, The Lockman Foundation.

Chapter 8

1. The following material is excerpted from information available in an ISI booklet called *Reaching Students From the People's Republic of China*. For the complete booklet, order directly from ISI (see Appendix A).
2. This section is excerpted from the ISI training brochure by Dr. Wilson Awasu, *How to Share the Good News With Your African Friend*. Dr. Awasu was born and raised in Ghana, West Africa. For additional material about your African friend, order the complete brochure (see Appendix A). Some of the additional material covered in this booklet relates to Islam, a dominant religion in North Africa and sizable areas around the Sahara.

Chapter 10

1. *The Advising Quarterly* (Fall 1987), pp. 3, 5.
2. Clyde Austin, *Cross-Cultural Reentry: An Annotated Bibliography*. (Abilene, Tex.: Abilene Christian University Press, 1983).
3. Lisa Espineli-Chinn, *Think Home—A Practical Guide for Christian Internationals Preparing to Return Home* (Colorado Springs: International Students, Incorporated, 1987).

God's Desire:

Knowing Him Forever

God loves you and wants you to know Him forever.

The Bible Says:

"This is good, and pleases God our Savior, who wants all people to be saved and to come to a knowledge of the truth" (1 Timothy 2:3, 4).

"This is how much God loved the world: He gave his Son, his one and only Son. And this is why: so that no one need be destroyed; by believing in him, anyone can have a whole and lasting life" (John 3:16).

God wants us to know Him personally now and forever. But we have a problem.

Our Problem:

Broken Relationship

God created us to enjoy life and a friendship with Him. He did not force us to love and obey Him, but gave us a will and freedom of choice.

The first man and woman chose to disobey God and to go their own willful way. We still make this choice today. This results in our relationship with God being broken.

THE BIBLE SAYS:

"For all have sinned and fall short of the glory of God" (Romans 3:23).

"But the trouble is that your sins have cut you off from God" (Isaiah 59:2).

Throughout history, individuals have tried many ways to make themselves acceptable to God ... without success.

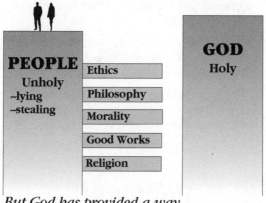

PEOPLE
Unholy
–lying
–stealing

Ethics

Philosophy

Morality

Good Works

Religion

GOD
Holy

But God has provided a way ...

God's Solution:

Jesus Christ

Jesus Christ is the only solution to this problem. The Bible says the final result of our disobedience is the penalty of death (Romans 6:23). By dying on the cross, Jesus took our punishment on Himself and made the way for our relationship with God to be restored.

THE BIBLE SAYS:

"For there is one God and one mediator between God and men, the man Christ Jesus" (1 Timothy 2:5).

"But God demonstrates his own love for us in this: While we were still sinners, Christ died for us" (Romans 5:8).

"The next day John saw Jesus coming toward him and said, 'Look! There is the Lamb of God who takes away the world's sin!'" (John 1:29).

God has provided the way. Will you accept it?

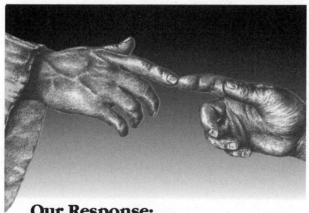

Our Response:

Receive Christ

We must place our trust in Jesus by accepting the payment for our sins that Jesus paid for us on the cross. If we give our lives to Him, then we can have a right relationship with God.

THE BIBLE SAYS:

"Look at me. I stand at the door. I knock. If you hear me call and open the door, I'll come right in and sit down to supper with you" (Revelation 3:20).

"Jesus answered, 'I am the way and the truth and the life. No one comes to the Father except through me'" (John 14:6).

"But to all who received him, he gave the right to become children of God. All they needed to do was to trust him to save them" (John 1:12).

Would you like to take this step today?

Beginning with Christ

Is there any good reason why you do not want to invite Jesus Christ into your life right now?

"I am the gate; whoever enters through me will be saved. He will come in and go out, and find pasture" (John 10:9).

Steps to a new relationship with God:

1. Admit your condition. (I disobeyed God and broke my relationship with Him. This is called "sin.")

2. Be willing to turn from your sins (repent).

3. Believe that Jesus Christ died for you on the cross and rose from the grave.

4. Through prayer, invite Jesus Christ to come in and control your life through the Holy Spirit. (Receive Him as Lord and Savior.)

The Bible Says:

"If you confess with your mouth, 'Jesus is Lord,' and believe in your heart that God raised him from the dead, you will be saved" (Romans 10:9).

Example of what to pray (make it your prayer)

Dear Lord Jesus,

I know that I am a sinner and need Your forgiveness. I believe that You died for my sins. I want to turn from my sins. I now invite You to come into my life. I trust You as Savior and follow You as Lord.

Thank you, Lord, for saving me. Amen.

_____

Date

_____

Signature

God's Assurance:

His Word

If you prayed this prayer,

THE BIBLE SAYS:

"For, 'Everyone who calls on the name of the Lord will be saved'" (Romans 10:13).

"For it is by grace you have been saved, through faith—and this not from yourselves, it is the gift of God—not by works, so that no one can boast" (Ephesians 2:8, 9).

Did you sincerely ask Jesus Christ to come into your life? If so, He has promised to do so. What has He given you?

THE BIBLE SAYS:

"So whoever has God's Son has life; whoever does not have his Son, does not have life. I have written this to you who believe in the Son of God so that you may know you have eternal life" (1 John 5:12, 13).

Walking with God

This is the beginning of a wonderful new life in Christ. To deepen this walk with Christ:

- Read your Bible every day to get to know Christ better.

- Talk to God in prayer every day.

- Be guided by the Holy Spirit.

- Tell others about Christ.

- Share your new life by your love and concern for others.

- Find another Christian or two with whom you can pray and share regularly your successes and failures.

- Worship and serve with other Christians in a church where Christ is preached.

God bless you as you do.

*God created people in His own image to
love Him and have fellowship with Him.
Jesus claimed He was the only way to
God. He was either a lunatic, a liar,
or who He said He was, the Lord God.
Jesus claimed many other things
about Himself:*

I am the living water (John 4:10–14).
I am the way, the truth, and the life (John 14:6).
I am the bread of life (John 6:35).
I am the light of the world (John 8:12).
I am the Good Shepherd (John 10:11).
I am the Son of God (Matthew 27:43).
I am the gate (John 10:9).
I am the vine (John 15:5).

Who do you say that He is?

P.O. Box C
Colorado Springs, CO 80901
Tel.: (719) 576-2700
Fax: (719) 576-5363
E-mail: ISITEAM@aol.com

Sharing Christ's Love with International Students

©1995 International Students, Inc.
Original material taken from "Knowing God" by Billy Graham
Evangelistic Association

Scripture references taken from:
The *Holy Bible, New International Version,* ©1973, 1978, 1984
International Bible Society.
The Message, Eugene Peterson, ©1993 Eugene Peterson.
The Living Bible, ©1971 Tyndale House Publishers.
The New American Standard Bible, ©1977 The Lockman Foundation.